A PRAYER FOR THE WORLD

GEORG F. VICEDOM

A PRAYER FOR THE WORLD

The Lord's Prayer — A Prayer for Mission

Translated by Edward and Marie Schroeder

CONCORDIA PUBLISHING HOUSE

SAINT LOUIS

Concordia Publishing House, Saint Louis, Missouri

Concordia Publishing House Ltd., London, E. C. 1

© 1967 Concordia Publishing House

Library of Congress Catalog Card No. 67-18122

Translated by permission from the original German

Gebet für die Welt, published by Chr. Kaiser Verlag, Munich, 1965

Contents

1. Prayer for the World   1
2. Mission and Prayer   13
3. The Our Father as a Mission Prayer   25
4. The Mission of God in the Our Father   45
5. The Action of God in the Our Father   83
6. For Thine Is the Kingdom . . .   129
7. The Prayer for Mission   141
Bibliography   167

26129

1. Prayer for the World

Mission and prayer is a subject we cannot consider without becoming personally involved. Should we push out into the open what is supposed to happen only in secret? On the other hand, prayer life as well as faith life is dependent on outside impulses and suggestions that can come only from those who pray and believe. Assistance is there both for faith and for prayer. As Christians, therefore, we have the opportunity to give one another assistance that can make our prayers in public worship more joyful, our home devotions richer, and our personal prayers more wholesome in practice. Paul was conscious of such aid to prayer, and so in all his letters he informed the congregations of his own prayer life.

We can hardly pray aright for the church's mission if we do not know what that mission is and what needs arise within it. We could distill such information from newspapers and books, but a short introduction will nevertheless be helpful.

Mission means being sent out into the world, a sending that can occur anywhere and everywhere. But when we speak of mission, we usually think of the work of our missionaries and mission societies, and it is of course necessary to support them with our prayers and offerings. But are we then really focusing on what God wants to do through mission? When we speak of mission, we must think of all the millions of people who have not yet found the way to Christ. From God's point of view they have a right to hear Christians proclaim the Gospel so they can come to faith in Jesus Christ and be gathered into His church through Baptism. How gigantic this task is can be seen in the fact that non-Christians outnumber Christians three to one. In addition, the world's population is growing so fast that world mission almost seems impossible if Christians do not use more of their forces to extend their faith.

Nowadays one often hears that the time for such face-to-face mission work is past. This is not true. Basically it is never past, for only through this work can a man be led to a decision for Christ. Revival areas where the Gospel is spreading very rapidly are Latin America, central Africa, southern India, Formosa, Korea, and New Guinea. Yet we should concentrate not so much on the great successes but much more on the quiet service that takes place everywhere as Christians contact non-Christians. It is through this that congregations steadily multiply. Mission, therefore, is not only a full-time professional vocation but everything Christians do to win non-Christians.

If we did not also understand mission to be the witness of the whole church, we could no longer speak of world mission. Political changes have made it impossible for missionaries to enter large sections of the globe. This applies to the whole area ruled by communism, especially to China, which used to be a great mission land. In other countries, such as India or Indonesia, great difficulties must be resolved in obtaining visas. The missionaries stand before closed doors. What good is a church's will for mission if it can find no opportunity for work? This makes it perfectly obvious to Christians: *We always have to do our work under the concrete conditions dictated by the course of world history.*

In spite of apparent peace, the world is full of turbulence and strife. Even where mission work is possible, it is often hindered and disturbed by social and political unrest. In many areas of South America and the centers of turmoil in Africa and Asia the work has become difficult. The strength of the Christian church in mission work has to prove itself today in her patient waiting, in the vulnerability of her life and service, but also in her certitude and hope that God as the Lord of history is leading her to His goal. Even in these difficulties God requires that His church obey and be faithful, demonstrating in her suffering that she is His flock.

Even under normal conditions it is no longer self-evident that mission work is carried out by a missionary from the Western world. Political changes among nations have taken away the white man's privileged position. Everywhere he encounters difficulties in making contacts. The people constituting the audience for the Western missionary's proclamation regard him with mistrust. The revival of non-Christian religions has set their followers in resistance to the Gospel. They try to prevent any further extension of the Christian church. Controversies arise and hinder the proclamation. Mission suffers discrimination because it is regarded as an extension of the white man's religion and as a remnant of colonialism.

But the situation is not hopeless, for these occurrences call people to a decision, especially when the Gospel is being extended by the local church. *The missionary must fit himself into the local church and work in cooperation with it.* In such a situation he too may experience the power of the Gospel among men. It is significant that where our missions abroad have been merged with the mission of the local churches they achieve greater success than those that have tried to maintain their independence. It is therefore imperative that our missionaries abroad live in brotherhood with other Christians. Theoretically this has long been clear but still difficult to carry out. We at home are not completely blameless in this respect. To a great extent we still consider mission as our own monopoly and not as the whole church using all her resources to extend herself. It does not even enter our head that the churches in Africa and Asia, simply by the mere fact of their existing in a non-Christian environment, have a call to mission. The best we can do is to join them in the work that God is accomplishing through them.

We must therefore be prepared to strengthen these churches. This does not mean financial support alone. The young churches expect much more from us. *They want us to supply people who will share with them something of our spiritual life.* To fulfill their servant role in the context of social and national upheaval, they need workers in all vocations. Yet these should be not merely experts in their fields but also conscious Christians, who

4

in the midst of their culture would be living examples to them of what following Christ should be. The young churches also need encouragement for their work. They need to be surrounded by the security of belonging to the whole Christian family; therefore they seek fellowship with us, which should express itself not least of all in intercessory prayer.

Aside from this mission work via individual effort there are many other tasks today that can no longer be done by a single mission or church. Ecumenical cooperation is urgently necessary. The world has grown small by virtue of the vast technical possibilities for communication. Nations and churches have the same needs and problems. We live in a great fusion of cultures in which all nations are interdependent, sharing with one another the best that they themselves possess. Assistance in technical development is certainly not the only area involved. Mighty spiritual forces wrestle with each other for influence over people. Not the least of these are the non-Christian religions. The path the world takes is, to a much greater degree than we care to admit, a spiritual process. In such a situation shall we Christians retreat? These facts present us with great possibilities for extending the Gospel.

For example, the pastors of the younger churches must be so trained that they can fulfill the Gospel's commission in this concrete world. This is possible only through unified planning in an ecumenical context. Every nation today wants to follow the so-called Western pattern. The key to this, as they understand it, is education. And rather than build schools, which the state can also do, it is more important to produce literature permeated with the Christian spirit. The printed word still has great power. Then there is radio broadcasting. The "Voice of the Gospel" station (in Ethiopia) can already reach a billion people. The huge correspondence coming in as a result of these broadcasts brings new opportunities. We must help shoulder the burden of these great tasks, for inherent in them is the temptation to understand mission falsely. God wants us to use such instruments, but we must see to it that they are used in the spirit of the Gospel.

Mission, therefore, is much more inclusive than we have understood it to be. We must hold before our eyes the vision of the whole world with all its unredeemed humanity, and the whole church as well. *God's mission always proves to be greater than our mission work.* God still has possibilities when men no longer see any. We must therefore adapt ourselves obediently to fit into His work. We can do this only in prayer. He does not bind us so completely to traditional kinds of work that we cannot take up something new. We should always be prepared for whatever He gives us to do. Neither dare we think of mission any longer solely under the special heading of missions to the heathen. God wants to save all men; therefore the church must proclaim the Gospel to the whole world.

In 1963 the World Missions Conference in Mexico discussed "Mission on Six Continents." Since modern unbelief has spread so far, there is no nation anymore that is not mission country, and there is no church group anywhere that does not find itself in mission country. That is why the church cannot possibly consider herself anything but a sent, missionizing church. On the one hand she must so preach the Gospel among her own people and so live her own life that the surrounding world may be called to decision; and on the other hand she must send emissaries out into the world so that the Gospel can be preached among all nations. The more the church conveys a missionary spirit to her own people, the more strength they will have for their sending; and the more they participate in missions to the heathen, the more joyfully they will carry out their service to the unbelievers in their own ranks. The two cannot be divided. We can no longer carry on mission heedless of the church's total life. Mission lives only by the power of faith, which God grants His church. That is why mission sets into motion in the church that which a church oriented to herself cannot begin to take up. Thus mission contributes to the renewal of life in the church. This fruit of mission in a missionizing congregation, however, will not grow unless the congregation prayerfully tries to discern God's redemptive will and to become an instrument of the Holy Spirit in the world. Mission without prayer is unthinkable.

The subject "Mission and Prayer" is only one of the many facets of prayer as they appear in the Holy Scriptures and the prayer literature of the church. We choose this limitation because there is already adequate literature about the other aspects of prayer. We probably cannot completely avoid saying much that applies to prayer in a general way, but on the other hand we also presuppose much that would otherwise have to be said. We will not consider the associations between faith and prayer or prayer and promise. And we are consciously not searching for the validation of prayer nor for its meaning since the believing man has never sought to justify his praying in any scientific sense. What authorizes prayer comes only from God, not from men or from scientific proofs. We will limit ourselves therefore to the associations between mission and prayer.

7

If we are to restore to our churches a genuine enthusiasm for mission, we must begin with the most elementary aspect of the Christian life, one in which every Christian can participate to extend the Gospel. Every Christian can take to heart the lost condition of men and place it upon the mercy of God that He may remove it by the good news of the Gospel. Everything in the Holy Scriptures points to this as God's goal. That is why the church's prayer life, when not tied in with mission, is just as much out of order as is the church's work when it does not orient its own congregational edification ultimately to extending the Christian faith. This gives the Christian's prayer its peculiar trademark — that he is also thinking of those who do not yet know God as their Redeemer. This gives it a distinctive dynamic because it gives the praying Christian a share in God's activity among men. If we want to describe this, we must try to expose the very heart of prayer. Here we are moving into unexplored territory, for Richard Handmann's small volume on the subject, *Das Gebet als Missionsmacht* (Prayer as Mission Power), (1912), does not go beyond the well-known statements about prayer. The correlation of mission and prayer must still be brought to light.

Since Christendom's mission task today is greater than ever, the work that lies before us is *urgent* — particularly because so few people perceive it to be so. For many it is surely old-fashioned. It would be much more modern to speak of equality and cooperation among all religions. It would also be more contemporary to speak of private aids for personal life, such as meditation, the practice of yoga, psychotherapy, and other things that modern man has substituted for prayer. The times we are living in are impoverished as far as prayer is concerned.

8

One of the causes for this, and surely not the least, is the substantive erosion of the Christian faith in God. *The more profound our knowledge of God, the greater our freedom and opportunity for prayer.* The less we are able to say about God, the less content our prayers will have. Man can still perhaps meditate on himself, as the Hindus and Buddhists do in their understanding of being, but he can no longer pray to a "Thou," a personal God. A man can pray only when he takes God seriously as his vis-à-vis and as Lord of the whole world. No one can pray to an idea or a principle, but only to an acting and working God. Whoever does not know the riches of "The one eternal God" knows nothing of his own poverty. Whoever is unaware of the power of the Almighty does not recognize his own weakness. Whoever does not acknowledge anything as the will of God avoids the embarrassment of needing direction — and thus man always remains master. Prayer, however, actually presupposes that God is real and that we can know Him by faith.

Perhaps Christianity's mission situation is so difficult because it no longer dares to determine the course of history through its prayer life and to let God be master in all things. Where among us are the Christians who will fold their hands while reading the newspaper, who are so grieved by the increasingly evident pervasiveness of sin, by the power of violence, by social injustice, and by moral indifference that they will pray for God's intervention? Where are the Christians whose intercessions accompany everything that is done to relieve these extremities? Do we still realize that every work of the church touches historical events?

Similar situations occasionally arose in the New Testament, and yet we read very little of any despair, uncertainty, or helplessness in the Christian community. It was a community constantly under attack, and it maintained its strength above all through its prayers. We, however, have already made success such a criterion of the correctness of our faith that any setbacks and opposition lead us to doubt the ways of God and to fall into fatalistic indifference. One has the impression that when difficulties increased in the New Testament congregations, so also did their joy in prayer. Early Christianity knew that God was still at work even when no success was in sight and that He still proved Himself the living God when He acted in judgment. He would exist even if there were no world, on the basis of whose natural laws we try to deny Him. That is why the early Christians did not simply write off what was now and then wrenched from their hands. They placed it into God's hand and thereby turned prayer into a mission tool, overcoming by prayer a world hostile to God. They became God's co-workers by putting their trust in His omnipotence at the very point when human judgment could expect nothing more. The conviction that God proved Himself to be their God, even when enemies attacked, gave them the power of hope.

Thus we recur once more to the thought that the prayer life of Christians is inseparably connected with their understanding of God. Non-Christians usually pray to local or functional gods. They invoke special powers, "experts in their field," to solve their problems. By defining the functions of their gods according to their concept of divinity they restrict the area of effectiveness of the gods. But the God who has revealed Himself in Holy Scripture manifests Himself as the one, absolute, all-encompassing God, unlimited in His power and unrestricted in His activity. Neither, according to His self-revelation, is He dependent on man's understanding of Him, nor has He any need of being confirmed by man's concept of God. He is God by Himself. There is nothing that is not subject to Him. He is the God of His creation and has always revealed Himself as the God of all men, even when He spoke and acted only with His own people. He is not a helper in emergencies nor a human stopgap but the God who holds His world in His hands and who shapes the course of history even when we do not always see or understand His governing hands. Only on the basis of this self-revelation, which subjects the understanding of God to no human limitations, can the joy and certainty of prayer arise.

Through prayer we are granted a share in God's work with the world and with men. Prayer, therefore, can encircle the whole world, it can move the whole world. Is it not true that the prayers of Christians are so often impotent and impoverished simply because they no longer dare believe God's comprehensive magnitude manifest in His self-revelation? They have transformed God into a God of the Christians and very often have degraded Him to the role of a national God. But God would not be God if He were not the God of all men. *The true understanding of God grants a worldwide perspective.* A Christian can never view the world except in this context because the whole world is subject to God, and history subject to Him can be understood only as universal history. Understanding God in this way also gives prayer its worldwide perspective. Just observe once that little word "all" in the prayer instructions of 1 Timothy 2:1-2: ". . . for *all* men, for kings and *all* who are in high positions." Christians can also appropriate a certain kind of worldwide perspective through educational media, but they do not discover the proper historical relationships of world events apart from faith in the one God to whom both heaven and earth belong. Only from such a faith can they relate everything to God. In their prayers they place the world at God's feet so that He may be its Lord. God is not a nebulous something that can be vaguely surmised, but on the basis of His revelation in Jesus Christ He is a God who loves the world, a planning, willing, working person who can be recognized when we believe in Him and experienced when we pray to Him.

2. Mission and Prayer

God has a plan for the world. Holy Scripture describes it as the rescue of men through Jesus Christ. Through the redemption God wants to bring men back from estrangement to be His creation and His possession and to transfer them to His kingdom. Thus He wants to become their God again, and they are to be His people.

God is the Lord of men, therefore, not only on the basis of creation. He is also their Redeemer, who through the death of His Son has made them His own once more. For many the redemption that took place in Jesus Christ is a scandal. God could probably have found other ways to rescue men. But since He traveled the way of the cross through His Son, we must accept this way as the strongest expression of His love to mankind. It is part of the very essence of God that He may also dictate to men just how He wants to have them redeemed. He has not left it up to men to decide whether and how they wish to be saved. Neither has He made humans so perfect that they could redeem themselves. He says to mankind, "I have redeemed you!" If God had allowed men to think of Him according to their image, then He would also have had to allow them to search for their own ways of redemption. But since He is God independent of men, man is denied the option to seek a way to God by himself.

Whoever, therefore, has come to know God through His revelation can confidently trust Him for rescue. He is thus assenting to God in His innermost being. Whoever rejects the redemption through Jesus Christ also separates himself from God. If there were still other ways of redemption, there would also have to be other gods, which would result in the ultimate conclusion that there can be no God. Men would be at the mercy of all sorts of powers. But through the redemption that took place in Jesus Christ, God has revealed Himself as the God of all mankind; therefore the redemption He achieved must also be proclaimed to all mankind.

God's sole will is that all men should be saved and come to the knowledge of the truth (1 Tim. 2:4). That is the message of His revelation; mission therefore flows from the Gospel. The very content of the Gospel makes the Christian's faith not a sterile but a witnessing one. The Gospel animates the church to let God place her into His service of extending the message of salvation. God accomplishes His goal through the church. The church lives on nothing else than receiving salvation from God. Acting on His commission she is then privileged to proclaim this salvation to all who do not know it. She is thus giving to others what she has herself received. This activity is inconceivable without prayer. She must be animated to it by God's love and equipped for it by God's power. Only through prayer can God transform her into a vessel for divine activity.

The more serious the church is about her own redemption through Jesus Christ, the more she will recognize how all men need the message of salvation for their own rescue. The more willingly she accepts God's gifts, the more grateful she will become toward God. Gratitude, however, fills the Christian's heart with joy over the fact that he may place himself at God's disposal. *Justification of the sinner by grace for Christ's sake through faith can never justify the church's lack of mission or her poverty in prayer;* for it is God's will that this message of redemption be proclaimed to all men. "Against God we cannot pray; we can pray only on the basis of His will. The propriety and power of our prayer reside in the fact that in prayer we unite ourselves with God's will" (Schlatter, p. 272). From this quotation we can deduce an important ground rule of prayer: Christians cannot pray in order to withdraw from God but only to bind themselves even closer to Him and to subordinate themselves to His operations. Thus by becoming witnesses of His love they return to God the gifts He gave them through the Gospel.

In prayer God offers His people the grand opportunity to be set free from self-assertion and to unite themselves with His will. Mission would not be the mission of God if He did not will it and accomplish it among men through His church. How could the church step into the current that originates from God and become His instrument if she did not let prayer make her receptive to the authorization and the power to step into it? Since God ultimately carries out the mission Himself, He has granted His church the opportunity to share in His marvelous work by prayer. The promise implicit in prayer always implies the additional possibility of the miraculous. Mission would be vain effort if God did not see to it that His Gospel accomplished its goal through His Spirit.

Since God always uses Christians to achieve His goal with mankind, He has yoked together mission and prayer. Mission is always His gift to His church. Just as He constituted His Son a missionary and sent Him into our world, so now He sends His church as His gift to men. Thus He calls laborers into His harvest and sends them where He needs them to proclaim the Gospel among men. He does not do this without the cooperation of His church, to whom He has delegated the task of sending. The church can win emissaries of God's love only in the manner her Lord and Master chose and sent His apostles. Before choosing His disciples He went into solitude and besought His Father for apostles; just so should His people be united with God in prayer about the task of mission and under His guidance beseech Him for laborers.

The church should ask for as many workers as she needs to perform her service in the world. In this praying she acknowledges God as the Lord of the church and lets Him direct her in this sending (Matt. 9:37 f.; Luke 10:2). To be able to pray this way is not a matter of course, particularly in view of the mission of God. "The command to pray God for laborers in the harvest (Matt. 9:37 f.) because the laborers are too few must be seen for the total audacity it implies. According to the traditional view the harvest laborers are the angels sent out at the eschatological end of the age. For Jesus, however, the harvest time is now because the kingdom of God is arriving" (Ferdinand Hahn, p. 32). Through this intercession the church stands right where the Kingdom is breaking forth. Therefore the number of her missionaries, pastors, and diaconate personnel closely corresponds to the extent that she views herself to be both product and instrument of God's mercy, obeying His commission in the eschatological event. The shortage of these workers has less to do with trends of the times than with the church's understanding of her own servant role and with the spirit of prayer dependent on it. Wherever the church prays in conformity with the divine will, her prayer is also answered. In prayer she is already carrying out the mission.

God bestows on His church the emissaries whom He Himself wants to send into the world. By virtue of God's commission and His answer to her prayers she also receives the authority to select from among the other Christians the men and women whom God has called and chosen for His service. Even in this selection process she must be one with the will of God and follow after Him in accomplishing what He has already done for her. This too is possible only in prayer. Here she is also following a New Testament practice. The early church ascertained through prayer whom God wanted to send (Acts 1:24 f.; 6:6; 13:1-3). But it is of crucial importance that she pay as close attention as did the early church to the prerequisites for this calling and sending. God does not call just anyone who presents himself. The decisive elements were not knowledge and professional ability. Eligible to be called in the early church were those who had lived a life with the Lord, who had proved themselves in His service, and who had distinguished themselves in spirit and wisdom. The other church members had to bear witness to their Christian life. What the Lord had done to those chosen for service and their relationship to Him were therefore decisive.

The early church also carried out her *commissioning*

and sending with prayer. Here too she acted on the authority God had given her through the Spirit's direction (Acts 13:1-3). In this commissioning by the church we see first of all that anyone who has been called by God and who is prepared to enter His service must also enter the service of God's church. There is no such thing as a free-lance missionary. God carries out His mission by making it His church's mission. But it would be false to designate the church or the congregation as the master of the mission. The church is never the active subject of the sending except to the extent that she lets God use her for that purpose. In prayer and in carrying out the commission the church acknowledges that God the Lord is working through her. The significance of the concomitant laying on of hands is that the church is releasing one of her members for God's work and placing him at God's disposal. The member receives an assignment and is thereby commended to the grace of God (Acts 14:26). The church not only places him under God's protection and blessing but also lays him in God's hands so He can direct this servant. The emissary is not his own master. He is subject to God's leadership so that he may perform Gods' works (John 6:28). Thus in the execution of God's missionary commission God, His church, and the emissary must be viewed together.

In service a unity arises in which God remains the doer. This unified view can only be achieved in prayer. "Man does what God does; God does what man does" (Hans Asmussen, p. 10). The church cannot do this if she herself does not constantly inquire about the will of God, which He carries out through His emissaries. But neither can the emissary do this if he is not constantly listening to those who stand behind him in prayer. Both are related to each other under God. Only God determines what the emissary's service shall be. Thus with regard to her emissaries the sending church must always inquire about the will of God. This is especially true in the trials and difficulties that accompany the sending. The will of God can become hard for both partners when the emissaries must travel the path to martyrdom. With what right does the church remove her messengers from the will of God when times of suffering are imminent? Are they not her ambassadors whom she has commended to the grace of God? In this crisis situation it becomes evident that the sending church herself must wrestle for the proper knowledge of God's will so that even in times of tribulation she may remain sure of her authorization. Only in this way can she strengthen her emissaries and make them certain of their calling.

No sending agency can demand that its emissaries place themselves under God's direction if it is unwilling to place itself under His guidance in carrying on its work. We seem to have made it a basic principle that in every case God wants to preserve life, and in times of crisis we act accordingly. But God may consider the death of His servant much more significant than preserving his life. And we usually see the guiding hand of God in His directing our history, as we see it, in linear continuity. But God does not usually act in a way that continually corroborates us. He can also shatter our tradition if it stands in His way. After all we are not in the world for ourselves but subordinate to a goal that God is accomplishing with all of Christendom. We would be alienating ourselves from the total picture and making ourselves lords over God's work if we were not open to new directives. God requires of us in every situation, even on such as might cast doubt on our own history and practice, that we trust Him alone. It is a matter of His great goal, not of our survival or our position.

The work assigned to us will endure only if it remains God's work, no matter where history may lead (Matt. 15:13). God does not always confirm our missionary plans even if they appear very sensible (Acts 16:5 ff.; 18:9 f.). *We can walk along God's way only if in our prayers we let God also hinder what we may have undertaken for Him.* He may deny us something that we might gladly have begun as a favorite project. He may lead us down strange ways. Paul did not reach Rome via the route he had prayed for (Rom. 1:10). He could not straighten things out in Thessalonica no matter how much he prayed (1 Thess. 3:10). Sending, therefore, entails not only action but also a tamed will and an inner discipline that grows only from prayerful familiarity with God. It should be the desire of all mission leaders and their emissaries to be able to echo what Jesus said at the return of the 70 disciples: "Yea, Father, for such was Thy gracious will." (Luke 10:21)

Although the church by the laying on of hands commends her emissaries to God and thereby foregoes the right to direct them, she still does not cut herself off from them. They remain her members because they have come out of her midst and because they are carrying out God's commission in her stead. What they do is her work. Whatever happens to them touches herself. She therefore participates in everything and bears their way of life with them. She shares their cares and needs, their problems and sufferings, but also their victories and joys. *They always remain embedded in the church — even when far removed from her.* The missionary without the church's backing is like an outpost without the protection of the troops. This connection can be maintained only by mutual exchange of news, strengthening, and intercession for each other. Through such intercession the church stands behind her emissaries and keeps herself conscious of her sending and her commitment. By praying for her emissaries her eyes remain turned toward the unredeemed world. She prays for the free course of the Gospel and for the blessed service of her emissaries. She places herself on God's side even when everything seems in vain so that the Gospel may be glorified also in tribulation (2 Thess. 3:1). Through intercession she participates actively in the inevitable confrontation with evil men when the Gospel is proclaimed. She prays that her emissaries may not become weak in the battle (Rom. 15:30 f.; Phil. 1:19 ff.; Heb. 13:18). The church's prayer can open closed doors (Col. 4:3). A praying church does not simply support the mission or merely view the battle. The ultimate responsibility always receives expression in prayer. While sharing this responsibility before the world, she is losing herself in God.

Through prayer the church also participates in the final goal of mission. The church becomes a partner in the hymn of praise sung by the redeemed community. *She glorifies God because even today He shows Himself as the saving God among men.* The mission leads those who have not honored God (Rom. 1:21) to praise Him. Thus the church is able to experience something of the joy the angels express in their praise to God when sinners repent (Luke 15:7). It is the community of forgiven sinners that constitutes the community before God's throne, eternally worshiping and proclaiming God's praise (Rev. 5:11 ff.; 7:9 ff.). Thus the church militant and the church triumphant are united in prayer, which not only encircles the world but also encompasses heaven and earth, and because it leads to the accomplishment of God's will, it animates the entire world.

The powerful events set in motion by prayer are unthinkable without the *working of the Holy Spirit,* through which God constantly agitates His people and leads them to work. The Spirit makes God's church willing to assume its missionary task. He calls the emissaries and through them proclaims the Gospel. He binds Himself to Word and Sacrament and turns the hearts of men to God. He gathers the church together, then leads her to witness. It is the Holy Spirit, then, who alone produces a genuine mission life. That is why Jesus found it very important for His disciples to wait for the gift of the Spirit and to prepare themselves with prayer to receive Him. (Luke 24:49; Acts 1:4; 1:14)

Genuine prayer life in the church is also unthinkable without the collaboration of the Holy Spirit, who is after all the Spirit of prayer (Luke 11:13). When the missionizing church receives the Holy Spirit, He actually begins praying with her, representing her. Through Him she can call upon God in all the distress and the difficulties and embarrassments that arise from the mission task. Through Him the church becomes genuine vis-à-vis God. She is liberated from her own will. She can worship God in spirit and truth (John 4:23). "Without the Spirit our prayer is the child of our own desires, mingling its dreams with our prayer and clothing God in our own wishes" (Schlatter, p. 183). Also in prayer the Holy Spirit is a Spirit of power and love and self-control (2 Tim. 1:7). He declares to the Christians what has already been given them and shows them what they need in order to do God's work (John 16:13 f.). He assures them of their sonship so that they place their complete trust in God, who has become their Father in Jesus Christ (Rom. 8:15;

Gal. 4:6). The Holy Spirit cares for the church and her emissaries and represents those who in their inner distress no longer know how they should pray since they no longer see the way God has set out for them. He cries out for them the "Abba! Father!" (Rom. 8:26). Thus in prayer He leads the church out of her helplessness and directs her eyes to God's goal. Under His direction it is impossible to pray and act against the will of God. Under Him, therefore, Christians are set free for God.

3. The Our Father as a Mission Prayer

What we have discussed so far about mission and prayer ought to be expanded and developed in several directions. We have foregone this because in the Our Father we have *the* mission prayer, which can tell us much better than any other passages how Christian faith, mission, and prayer are interrelated.

It will surprise many that we designate the Our Father a mission prayer and not a prayer of the church, as it is usually interpreted. It is that too, of course. *It is the prayer of the missionizing church.* In the Our Father we can discern in a unique and singular fashion that the church of Jesus in her total prayer life can be understood only as a missionizing church. When Jesus' disciples asked their Master to teach them to pray according to His own example and the practice of John the Baptist, as recorded in Luke 11:1, He presented them with the Our Father. Thereby He gave them the prayer that has since bound all Christendom together in its faith and service. The disciples were Jesus' church of that time. This church consisted of men whom He had called personally to follow Him so that He could send them into the world of unbelief as apostles of His Gospel. Matthew conveys this even more strongly than Luke. According to him, Jesus taught His disciples to pray and through this very prayer placed them in contrast to the Jews (Matt. 6:5 f.) and the pagans (6:7). He gave them a prayer containing not only the new relationship with God but also the new faith He had granted them. He taught it to men whom He had already called the salt of the earth and the light of the world (5:13-16). They possessed something through the Gospel that other men did not have but which they needed for their salvation.

The Our Father is therefore an apostolic prayer. It is given to disciples whom the Lord Himself sends out (Matt. 10:5) and to whom He also gives the great missionary commission after His resurrection. Jesus teaches men whose work joins them to His own sending (John 20:21) and whom He has called to continue His work on earth to pray. It is a small community of men for whose faith, obedience, and witness Jesus Himself has prayed to the last hours of His life so that through their preaching the world might be saved and His Father glorified (John 17). The Our Father thereby constitutes the disciples a missionizing, praying group united by prayer even when their service disperses them among the unbelievers. Praying to their one Father binds them together.

If today we understand the Our Father primarily as the prayer of the church, this does very likely convey its essence. But in terms of its origin it remains a constant question to the church's understanding of herself. Does she still pray it as a congregation conscious of her mission task and of her special place in the world? Does she still live in the conviction that she is called to offer men rescue through Jesus Christ? Or does she misinterpret the Lord's Prayer so selfishly that God's loving will for all mankind is no longer evident? As children of the heavenly Father we are of course allowed to pray the Our Father also in such a way that we thank Him for this privilege, but we must not forget that children of the Father are always disciples of Jesus, who are to continue the work for which He was sent. If we are not disciples of Jesus, neither do we then have any right to claim sonship. But if we are children, then Jesus has also made us witnesses to His Gospel, and He gives us a missionary calling.

The Our Father becomes a mission prayer above all by its very content. It is the shortest presentation of the Biblical and thus also the missionary message that we have in the Holy Scriptures. "As a matter of fact, the Lord's Prayer is the clearest and, in spite of its terseness, the most comprehensive summary of Jesus' proclamation which we possess" (Jeremias, p. 16; see also Schniewind, *Das Evangelium des Matthäus,* "Das Neue Testament Deutsch," p. 78). It expresses the decisive elements of what Jesus proclaimed and what has become different in our relationship with God through Him. God's saving intention permeates every petition. Through the Our Father we leave the acceptance and the completion of salvation to Him who in Jesus Christ began the work of sending. Whoever understands the Our Father in its fullness has the missionary message. Whoever prays the prayer in its original meaning is also prepared to pass on to other men what Jesus brought. He joins himself to the work of Jesus and lets the Father on whom he calls control him. He would be a hypocrite if he denied himself to

27

God while asking Him for the fullness of salvation described in the message of the Our Father.

Through the Our Father Jesus also makes a clear separation, or rather differentiation, between Himself as the content of the message and those who are to proclaim it. Nowhere in the New Testament do we find that Jesus prayed together with His disciples. He probably participated in the Jewish worship services together with them, and He did spend whole nights in prayer. Yet *unfortunately nothing is reported to us about a common prayer of Jesus with the disciples.* Even in His last hours, when He admonishes His disciples to watch and pray, He separates Himself a stone's throw from them to pray alone (Matt. 26:39; Mark 14:35). It is as if they should not be permitted to hear what He has to say to the Father alone. He has given His disciples the proper prayer in the Our Father, but He has not united Himself with them in it. Jesus always prays, "My Father," and He teaches His disciples to say, "Our Father." He differentiates between "My Father" and "your Father." Thereby He makes a clear distinction between Himself and His disciples, a distinction that has its foundation in the two separate relationships with the Father. He is the One who has come from the Father and who returns to the Father, being one with the Father. The praying community, however, is a community of forgiven sinners who have found their way to the Father through Him. Jesus has no need of first establishing His relationship to the Father. Whoever sees Him sees the Father. He is the Son, while His disciples become children only through Him. Thus even in prayer He remains the Lord and Master.

If Jesus had united Himself in prayer with His disciples, He could not have become the object of their worship. If His prayer needs had been the same as theirs, people could scarcely have accepted Him as Redeemer. But He was the Redeemer, and they were the redeemed. Therefore after His resurrection He was Himself worshiped. We know that even the early church prayed to her Lord and Head. She had no need to carry out any process of deification, for He had revealed Himself as the Son of God. His deity shone through His humanity.

For the Jews the doctrine of His being God's Son was the great heresy. It was because of his zeal for the Jewish faith that Paul persecuted those who called upon the name of Jesus (Acts 9:14). After his conversion Ananias admonished him to pray to Jesus (22:16). Praying to Jesus became common also in the Gentile Christian communities. Paul greeted those who called on the name of the Lord Jesus Christ (1 Cor. 1:2). To them he wished the peace that Jesus Christ had brought (2 Tim. 2:22). Christians, therefore, differed from other men because they honored Jesus Christ as their Lord and God. That He nevertheless taught His followers to pray to the Father is quite in line with His work, which was to be nothing else but what He saw the Father do.

Prayer to Jesus nevertheless originated already with Him. According to John, He directed them to pray in His name. "When the Lord's Prayer was given to the disciples, prayer in Jesus' name began (John 14:13-14; 15:16; 16:23)," (Jeremias, p. 16). To pray in Jesus' name means to pray as one who consents to the petitions of the Our Father and acknowledges Jesus' work of redemption. Men who pray in this way belong together under Him. Through His death He cleared their way to the Father. Prayer in Jesus' name acknowledges the love of God for men. *Praying in Jesus' name is glorifying the Father,* who sent His Son into the world. On the other hand, prayer in Jesus' name is not to be separated from prayer to Jesus

29

Christ Himself. Whoever prays in Jesus' name prays to Jesus Himself and acknowledges His position as mediator. Praying to Jesus Christ, therefore, is not worshiping another God, but through Him it is the honoring of the Father who gave His Son for the rescue of men. It is the glorifying of the redeeming God (John 14:13; 15:7 f.; 16:23 f.). It is to Him that the church turns in the Our Father — always the Father of our Lord Jesus Christ.

We are given two forms of the Our Father in the New Testament, a short form in Luke and an expanded form in Matthew. It is not necessary that we here take up the consideration as to which is the original. Whoever wants detailed information can check Ernst Lohmeyer or Joachim Jeremias. For the praying man it is important to know that the short form is contained in the longer form with only minor textual differences. We have therefore not two Our Fathers but one. When we say the Our Father, we pray the words that the Lord taught His disciples and which have been delivered to us through two church traditions. The varying forms indicate that in the early church the Our Father was not understood as a stiff, firmly fixed prayer. In its very form it was a living conversation with the Father, just as it should be for us.

The significance of the Our Father as mission prayer goes far beyond what has already been said. Since it contains Jesus' proclamation in the most compact form, *it was used above all as teaching material in instruction for baptism.* By means of the Our Father the catechumens were led into the mysteries of the Christian faith. Through the Our Father baptismal instruction became prayer instruction. This has decisive significance. The prayer life of Christians is dependent to an important degree on their familiarity with what God has done for men. Only when they know the content of faith do their lips open to praise and give thanks. Only when they know how powerful God has shown Himself to be in the course of history, both in His love and in His judgment, does their trust in God find a basis enabling them to entrust everything to Him in prayer. Nowadays we have by and large eliminated the Our Father from instruction courses. This fact is characteristic of the attitude of contemporary Christians. We talk very much about God but very little with God because we do not allow God Himself to talk to us through His revelation. But whenever talk about God is not anchored in the speaking of God Himself and does not lead to a talking with God, everything remains empty no matter how significant it seems scientifically. The catechumens of the first centuries learned to know God in prayer, and thereby He became for them an intimate reality.

The missionary message of the Our Father is already given by the prayer's address, from which the missionary viewpoint of the individual petitions is derived. *Only when this address contains the full abundance of the biblical statements about God do the subsequent petitions also have meaning.* Scholars point out that addressing God with the name Father was common already in Judaism and was also practiced in pagan religions. They can also document the connection between the individual petitions and Jewish prayers (see also Gerhard Ebeling, pp. 48–49). To begin with, this removes none of the Our Father's originality. The results of scholarly research can only prove that Jesus was familiar with the Jewish prayer tradition. Since this had arisen from the true faith in God, everything expressed in the Old Testament about God also stands behind the Our Father. Moreover, the use of the name Father in the prayers of oriental religions need not disturb us. Even when this name was really used seriously, men still could not grasp its substance because it contradicted their understanding of God and man. Mohammed, for example, found the name Father the greatest insult to God. He made God so transcendent that He could no longer be described in terms of human relations. In the religions of India, which speak much of the unity of man with the divine, there can be no vis-à-vis of God to men. God therefore cannot be addressed as Father. Addressing God with the name Father is possible only when man stands vis-à-vis God and is allowed to bridge the chasm because God has bridged it.

Through Jesus Christ the name Father received new meaning. The god worshiped in oriental religions remained the absolute, distant lord whom no one ultimately had to take seriously because he did not bother about men. In the Judaism of Jesus' time the Jahwe whom they addressed as Father remained the God of their fathers and was worshiped as the God of Israel, *but Jesus through His proclamation gave new content to the name Father.* He first addressed God with "Abba" and thereby placed the father-child relationship in the center of the prayer. It is children who are praying to their Father — hence men who would have no existence without the Father. They are men who already stand on the Father's side and who are bound together with Him by their very existence. Thus in the name Father lies the message of creation. Jesus proclaimed the Creator God to be the loving Father. Between Him and His children is a life relationship, but not one that would pull God down to the human level and thus cast doubt on His Godhead. He is a God who is fond of His children and wills the best for them even when they do not want to recognize it. That is why the children may approach the Father in loving trust. This confidence in God is basically the new-ness of Christian prayer, which most strongly impresses especially the pagans.

Thus by using the address "Father," Jesus bound it together with the thought of childhood, thereby placing God and men in a special relationship to each other. By becoming man He gave this relationship meaning and content. He Himself came as the Son from the Father and became man so that men could become God's chil-dren. He was the embodiment of the new relationship with God. Whoever believes in Him and finds his way to God through the redemption granted by Him becomes a child of God. Thus He won for men the right to address God as Father.

Through His attitude toward the Father and through His proclamation Jesus has not, however, invali-dated or annulled the other attributes of God. God re-mains for Him the Creator and Lord. He remains the God who acts with men, who has revealed Himself in judgment and grace in the history of Israel. He is for Jesus the Lord of the whole world and of all men, and He remains for Him the God who will have a day of judgment for all nations. But Jesus has given the attri-butes revealed in God's acting and speaking a new rela-tionship to men, an orientation toward men that is per-meated with God's love and mercy. He has proclaimed God as the Father of all men and through His suffering has opened for all the way to the Father. And yet by using the name Father He has not invalidated the holi-ness of the name but has rather emphasized it by His rec-onciling death.

The early Christians did not forget this fact; that is why they prevented the Our Father from becoming a common prayer for the masses. They protected it like a treasure that must not be profaned by the pagans. *It was the prayer of Christians* because only they knew the content of the prayer through the divine revelation they had received. The pagans did not have the prayer taught them and explained by means of the Biblical proclamation until they had decided to become Christians. That is why, as long as early Christianity was a missionizing church, the Lord's prayer could not be used in public worship services open to the pagans. At such worship services the church used it only in the Communion liturgy after the pagans had been dismissed.

Because of our one-sided proclamation of the name Father, our exclusion of the Old Testament from the proclamation, or our hasty interpretation of it in terms of Christ, scarcely anything is said nowadays about the other attributes of God, and this has inevitably made God appear rather harmless. We no longer link the address with the first article of faith. We can hardly realize, therefore, what a jolt the religious world of Jesus' time suffered through the message that He laid down in the Our Father and what a privilege it was for the Christians to be allowed to call upon God as Father. They found this gift so frighteningly great in the context of their total understanding of God that they used the name Father only with sacred awe. How could wretched, sinful, creaturely man address the holy God, the Lord of heaven and earth, with the name Father and pull Him onto his own level? This was for them the incomprehensible thing that had happened through Jesus.

How easily we could explain so much of the early Christians' piety if we still had any feeling for this exciting and unbelievable condescension of God toward man! The early Christians had it. They guarded against using the Our Father in such a way that the name Father might be discredited. They were still conscious of the fact that only in full connection with the total understanding of God could individuals have the freedom to pray. They were also aware that only those disciples of Jesus who had come to the true faith in God possessed the right to say "Father" in this fashion. Therein lay the uniqueness of their faith vis-à-vis the Jews and the heathen. By using the Our Father they were simultaneously guarding the heart of their faith. Their reverence was so great that they introduced the Our Father, as we learn from the Chrysostom liturgy, by praying: "Make us worthy, O Lord, that we joyously and without presumption may make bold to invoke Thee, the heavenly God, as Father and to say, Our Father." (Translation from Jeremias, p. 17.) Similarly the Roman Catholic Mass says: "Admonished by salutary instruction and guided by divine teaching, we make bold to say, Our Father."

History teaches that neither in the Eastern nor in the Roman Catholic Church did this knowledge of the Christian's privilege prevent a misuse of the Our Father. It is all the more urgent, therefore, to return to a proper use of the Our Father. If in our prayers we do not remain conscious that God, whom we invoke as Father, is also our Lord and Judge, we can never achieve the proper prayer attitude. *Through His proclamation of the name Father Jesus did not invalidate the Godhead of the God revealed in Himself.* On the contrary, in His person God was present among men, in whose presence we also stand. He would also have been the last one to have dared replace the name God with the name Father and to becloud God's holy activity. But when Jesus describes God's intrinsic relationship to men, He uses the name Father. Thereby with Him the Father concept internally

35

permeates the name of God and gives it a particular direction for us.

Thus Jesus does not diminish God's lordship by using the designation Father, but He accentuates and emphasizes it in a very specific way. In it the believer learns of the full power of God, who by virtue of His fatherhood has proprietary rights over men. Jesus presents it as the content of childlike faith that God cares for us like a housefather or family father and keeps His household in order as its Master. God is Master of the house since He is Lord of all. His lordship is not confined to those who know Him as housefather and worship Him but extends over His entire creation. He preserves what He has called into life and nourishes all the children of men (Matt. 6:26). Since He is the Lord, He also knows what His children need before they ask Him (6:8). He is also the Lord of history, without whose will nothing happens. The sparrow on the roof and the hair on our heads are both encompassed by His fatherhood. How could He forget the rest of mankind? His actions are not limited to His church. He does indeed reveal Himself to His people and make them exemplify His love and grace, but they also exemplify His judgment. From their history we can deduce that neither has God released the pagans from His guidance and concern. He is not the God of the Jews or of the Christians, as His people have understood Him again and again in history. He is so much the Lord of the universe that He is not dependent on His church. He can also raise up children for Himself from stones if His fatherhood is misused (Luke 3:8). He sends rain on the just and on the unjust (Matt. 5:44 f.). He determines the boundaries for the nations (Acts 17:26). His fatherhood is the source of all the families on earth (Eph. 3:14 f.). Thus all men belong to Him. Holy Scripture from its very first page testifies that God is the Lord of the whole world. Yet we act as though He must first give us an account of His existence. What sort of God would that be? Only because God is the universal Lord is He also our God. Only from such an understanding of God does prayer acquire its full content and meaning.

The privilege of Christians is that they know of this one God. They have experienced His love through Jesus Christ and for His sake may call Him Father. They strip their prayer of its promise, however, when they confine its effectiveness to Christians. We diminish God when we forget in our praying that every act of calling upon Him is a confession to the Creator and Lord of the whole world from whom everything comes and in whom all things endure. *He is Lord of His entire house, which includes heaven and earth.* God in the heavens is also the Lord of the universe, in which the earth is but a segment of His concern and love. Thus our praying acquires its breadth. As Christians we can pray only as members of a total mankind that has already been embraced by the love of God since He had His Son die for it. We are united with mankind by creation since all mankind was created for God. We belong together with mankind by virtue of Christ's death since He died for all men. In this God-given solidarity of Christians with non-Christians God's church gets a chance to be God's house in the pneumatic sense. Thus God's name as Father already urges mission since God's family, which has arisen by faith in Jesus Christ, serves to liberate the entire creation into the glorious liberty of the children of God, and it does this on the basis of the redemption wrought in Jesus Christ (Rom. 8:20 f.). Only when prayer is founded on such an understanding of God does it become a reality that moves the world. What we ask of God always places us into the area of God's action with total mankind. Only on the basis of God's fatherhood is there any brotherhood of men, for whom His Gospel is intended.

Since God sent His Son into His created world as Redeemer of all men, He has become Father in a special sense for those who believe in Him. He loved the whole world, but in His church this love becomes visible (John 3:16). The name Father is thus no attribute ascribed to God first of all by the Christians; its source is to be found in God's love for men. It was revealed to men by Jesus Christ and proclaimed after Him by the apostles. Jesus taught men to pray to the Father, and by the forgiveness of sins that He achieved He brought them the right to be God's children, which amounts to having access to God's heart. By His suffering and resurrection God's name of Father acquired a meaning, and by the preaching of Christ's Gospel it was protected from misuse. It is not as though we draw near to God in prayer and call Him Father on the basis of our prayer experience. On the contrary, *our praying is already a response to the revelation of His Father name* as Jesus taught it and the apostles preached it. Wherever mission is carried on the Father name is revealed anew to men. Praying therefore is not only speaking with God but first of all responding to His address and entering into His fellowship.

Christians are distinguished from the heathen by the fact that they have been granted to know that God has become their Father. Because He let His Son become man, we have become children; and through Him we live in fellowship with the Father. Our status as children therefore exists via the Son. It does not arise from any mystical piety of oneness with God, as Asian religions teach. Whoever denies the Son does not have the Father, and whoever confesses the Son has the Father too (1 John

2:23). To those who received the Son He gave power to become the children of God (John 1:12). Only through Him do we come to the Father. God's fatherhood is thus the primary factor. Were He not Father, we could not be children. Only through the Father do we acquire any new destiny for our existence, not through ourselves. Our status as children is therefore a gift and not a claim. Everything about it originates in the Father. He draws us to His Son so that we might become children (John 6:44). In Jesus Christ God remains the One doing the action. By the Father of our Lord Jesus Christ we have been born anew (1 Pet. 1:3). But those who have been born of God are children of God. He places them in the kingdom of His beloved Son (Col. 1:13). He qualifies us to share in the inheritance of the saints in light (Col. 1:12). We become fellow heirs with Jesus Christ (Rom. 8:17). God is our Father because He has accepted us as His children. Sonship is therefore both gift and prerogative. Since the gift is to be shared by all men, this constitutes the foundation stone for mission. The church of God becomes the example of what God intends for all men. But this also implies the responsibility to proclaim the gift to all men!

By means of sonship God wills to unite all who by virtue of creation belong to Him. Within creation the church constitutes the family of God that has found its way home; the rest of mankind is still living in the far country. Via sonship God as Father of the household transforms us into fellow members of His household (Eph. 2:19). Thus He leads those who from His vantage point live afar off, who have separated themselves from Him by sin, back to Himself, uniting them in His house as His church. This family of God is intended to be the one and only fellowship. Within it the chasm that separated it from God is eliminated. For this reason there must also be no separation within it. Just as it has only one Father, so there is only one sonship. It comes into existence by God's forgiving and accepting us. Through forgiveness the relations of the accepted to one another are kept in order. Just as forgiveness is the key to the Father's house, so it also brings the children of God together. Whoever does not maintain, receive, and grant fellowship on the basis of forgiveness with his God-approved brothers and sisters is excluding himself once more from the Father's house. Without forgiveness prayer does not get through to God (Matt. 6:14; Mark 11:25). By forgiveness all who believe in God are joined together in the Father's name. He keeps them all in His house despite all their differences in doctrine if they seek forgiveness and grant it, that is, if they seek to be nothing but children of the one Father.

By having received redemption, Christians are distinguished from all other men. Pagans and unbelievers still live afar off. Yet they too belong to the household of God even if they are not yet part of His family. To be sure, they still live separated from Him and dishonor His name, but in the last analysis they cannot break away from His lordship. Just as everything in sonship proceeds from Him alone, so also He alone determines whether He grants the others His love and concern or calls them up for judgment. God remains the Lord of all men; therefore they also belong to His household whether they will to be there or not.

John designates as the meaning of Jesus' sacrificial death the gathering of the scattered children of God into one (John 11:52). Although this passage initially means those who already stand in child relationship, it nevertheless calls our attention to the fact that the church of the

40

Crucified is a gathering place for those who will be called to God. The family of God therefore is fundamentally open for all who still stand far from it. The sonship procured by Jesus Christ would be meaningless if it were not intended for all men. God continues the gathering of His children by using those who can bear witness of the sonship. They are able to make the offer. This assignment must so animate the church that she sets as the goal for her praying the growth of God's family, or the sonship of all men.

The reference to location in the salutation of the Our Father is a scandal for many people today. *They see in these words a localization of God.* This appears to them vulnerable since scientifically there is no heaven in the sense of a permanent residence. It is also offensive for them since it expresses God's transcendence, which for modern man is intolerable. The localization is actually not essential and according to Luke could be dropped. But what would be gained thereby? The same persons not only oppose this offense to natural science but also every conception of God, even the concept and the name. Does anything like prayer then still exist? One can no longer pray to an "event," to a speaking, an occurrence, a process. One might still have awe in the face of such a reality, but a personal relationship to it is no longer possible. On the other hand there is scarcely a serious man of prayer who has ever searched or had to search for God in heaven since in prayer God came so close to Him that he was standing in His very presence. The genuine man of prayer does not have to speak of God as an event since in prayer something always happens to him by God's action. If a man believed he could overcome the problem of God's transcendence with the formula "God in the depths" and thus put men into the presence of God, this

41

would be a grand self-delusion. For "God in the depths" is also a localization of God and probably more difficult to comprehend than "in heaven." The latter at least still grants God's infinite and unlimited character and expresses His grandeur and power. "In the depths," however, turns God into an earth-god. If we are going to seek for a new way of addressing God, then at least it ought to be one that encompasses God's entire created realm. This, of course, is not the main point, but rather the knowledge that no man exists who is not living in the presence of God and that no place exists where God is not also present. Only in this way can we again succeed in shifting man's life and thought into God's light.

If the danger here is that a new doctrine of God would render any prayer impossible, there are two additional references which show that *Christians must retain the Biblical understanding of God precisely for the sake of prayer*. Christian prayer is different from the prayer of the Jews though both pray to the same God. Although the Jews never deny God's universality, they have nevertheless made Him into a God of Israel. They always pray in the consciousness that God has granted them a unique position in which they are accorded before all men a very special status with God. The prayer of Christians is also characterized by their relationship to God, but via sonship it takes on completely different characteristics. Christians are able to pray only as men who have been granted a very great gift. Therefore the fundamental tone of their piety is not election but thankfulness, which must find its expression in a humble heart, single-minded faith, and trust in the Father's love. They can bring nothing except their empty hands, which they daily let Him fill with new strength. They are not the possessors but the needy. This makes them inwardly rich.

Since they are so needy, they do not stand before God in their own right but in His love, which draws them to Him. For them prayer is the station before God where life is always refilled anew and whence everything is brought back to God as thanks and sacrifice since it belongs to Him. Christian piety therefore must be different from that of the Jews. (Matt. 5:20; 6:5 ff.)

Christians also pray differently from the pagans. They know of God's creativeness and give Him the honor, while the pagans despite their knowledge of God do not honor Him (Rom. 1:21). Since Christians know about the fatherly love, they may also trust God in external things (Matt. 6:32). They are able to praise God free from anxiety. They know God's fatherly will and align themselves with it. Consequently they are not agitated by the anxiety of life. Neither, therefore, do they make any use of prayer magic. They have the promise of eternal life directing their attention beyond their own lives. Therefore they have no need for storming God with many words for the sake of their own existence nor for pressing their own will upon Him with magic incantations. They know that they may pray for everything. Even the most insignificant thing is worth a petition, and even the greatest can still be put into words and brought before God.

4. The Mission of God in the Our Father

The Our Father is usually considered to have two sets of petitions. That is, the first three petitions refer completely to God, to His name, His kingdom, and His will; the last four petitions deal with man and his concerns. But we shall see that in the Our Father we cannot separate quite so clearly. What God claims for Himself in the first three petitions has eminent significance for men, and what the second portion prays for is most closely connected with the breaking forth of God's dominion. One could almost say it is a consequence of the actualization of the first petitions.

One thing, at any rate, is clear: the first three petitions refer to God's concerns, but they are directed toward the rescue of men; and since this is completely God's work, this rescue must also be asked of God. God's honor, His kingdom, and His will are means to salvation that He Himself uses. We learn about God's goal and hear about His motives. To carry them out, He Himself is constantly at work. All the petitions contain mission; therefore in view of our subject we are able to speak of the mission of God in the Our Father. Just as mission is solely God's action, which He began in Jesus Christ and continues today through His church, so also what we request of God in the first three petitions in reference to mission is solely His work, which He wills to translate into action through us.

Hallowed Be Thy Name

If the name Father contains everything we know about God on the basis of the revelation in Jesus Christ, then we can understand the early church for sensing a pious awe in using the Father name. They still perceived what an extraordinary thing was given them with the name Father. The holiness of God's name resided in the address "Father." When Jesus set up in the First Petition a protection for the name of God that reminds us of the Second Commandment in the Decalog, it is because He wanted to teach us that in our life and prayer we are in danger of humanizing God, making Him one of us. That is why we must pray that God Himself would keep His name as holy as He Himself is holy. This will be true only if we allow the holy God to make us holy also.

A name is always the expression of him who holds it. There is no name by itself. Behind every name hides a reality the name should disclose. *Whatever is predicated of a name always refers to the bearer of the name.* By proper use of a name someone is honored, by misuse he is insulted. The Jews knew of the mystery of the name. That is why they did not dare to speak the name of God but circumscribed it. Pagans often take a similar attitude. For instance, they dare approach their gods only with sacrifice because they are afraid to take a god's name onto their lips without a gift for him. A name represents the bearer. It carries with it the holiness of the one designated because the bearer defends his name.

Christians are allowed to use the name of God. Jesus Christ has granted them the freedom to pray to God without fear. He has brought the sacrifice. Unfortunately this has caused many to lose any awe before the name of God and to use it as if they could judge God and make Him justify Himself before them. Many treat the name Father in a way they would not dare use a human name. Such facts make it evident that the Christian's relationship to his God can be perverted much more easily than the heathen's. That is why this petition is directed primarily against the Christian's own carelessness. Every Christian should know that the First Petition inquires about his understanding of God.

The name of God is God's revelation to men, especially the name Father. A nameless god is no god. If God had not given Himself a name, we would know nothing of His being. Everything that God has done and is doing would remain in the darkness of man's forebodings if it were not disclosed through His name. Through it God exists for us; He is a reality we can experience. This does not mean that God exists only by the fact that He has a name; on the contrary, He gives Himself a name because He is a living God. He was there before the foundations of the world were laid, and He will still be God when there is no longer a creature around to speak His name. By giving us His name He speaks to us as the One who proceeds from Himself, the Existent One, taking hold of us and pulling us in His train. Without the revelation we would have at best an inkling of God's being, which we could not define any more closely. Through the revelation the name of God becomes clear. God comes close to us in His name. Through His name He becomes God among men, God for us.

Today there are theological trends that would like to make God nameless. They speak of a "Cipher God." They prefer not to accept and use as a gift the revealed name of God but would rather determine themselves what name a person could give to what he understands to be God. But every name-giving from the human side would necessarily lead to confusion because everyone would have to use a different name, each according to his own understanding. Finally there would be no more name of God. The essence of God would then stand no higher than any human way of understanding. It is indicative that today Christian theologians describe God only by His functions. They scarcely realize that they have thus adopted a structure of heathenism whereby the divine is divided into functions, but no "total picture" of God can arise. Prayer decides whether a man's understanding of God is right. God can be worshiped and honored only if His name is valid. A nameless god is meaningless for men. Perhaps an altar could be built to him, as in Athens. He could perhaps even be honored by sacrificial gifts. But any prayer to him would necessarily exhaust itself in clichés. No worship of God by prayer, praise, or thanksgiving would be possible because a nameless god cannot reveal himself through word and deed. *Whoever takes away God's name allows Him to sink into darkness and makes of Him a phantom.*

When we pray, we must call upon God by His name. The more this name holds of God's revealed actions, the richer will be our prayer potential, the greater our prayer certainty, and the more we will be grasped by God Himself. A nameless god cannot be so honored by men that they sense awe before his holiness. The way men associate with him is completely meaningless. But wherever the name of God is known through His revelation, it can be profaned, doubted, denied, voided, and dishonored. By revealing His name God stands at the disposal of men and gives Himself into their hands. That is why the petition for hallowing His name becomes a necessity. Men's responsibility before God arises from the name of God. They can place themselves in the service of this name or they can dishonor it.

The revelation of the name of God has therefore made it possible for men to profane, misuse, and despise it. That is why Jesus teaches His disciples to pray, "Hallowed be Thy name." It is not just any name that should be held in honor. Neither is any inordinate human ambition involved. The Our Father turns our eyes away from the claims of men and turns them toward God; for men forget that God can also expect something from men. This petition demands no more and no less than that we acknowledge God in His action and thank Him for it. When we pray "Thy name," we confess God, who has revealed Himself as the Lord of all men. We place ourselves on the side of Him who in Jesus Christ has become our Father. Thus we bring our daily life and our redemption into relationship with Him. God's name is so honored that we let Him be everything.

We do not intend here to go into the various meanings of the word "hallow" (to make holy). The holy is that which is set apart, invested with power, generating apprehension, dangerous. To "hallow" would certainly not mean that our actions are necessary to help God attain a dangerous abundance of power. The petition does not say, "You should hallow God's name." It uses the passive form: "Hallowed be Thy name." Thereby it expresses that "God's name by itself is already holy." *The name presides over its holiness by virtue of its own competence.* Holiness has such an effect on men that in it they are able to understand God's very nature. To hallow in this case would mean that they acknowledge the abundance of God's power, humble themselves before it, and guard against coming in contact with it since that would be the end of them. It is not this characteristic of the fearful that is decisive, however, but the fact that this holiness of God determines the meaning of the passive form of the petition. Hallowing takes place among men, but the impetus for it originates in God Himself since He permits them to experience His holiness. Thus in hallowing we are incorporated into a movement that has its ultimate source in God Himself. We are exposed to the effect of God's action, and so His name becomes holy for us.

Herewith we have already come upon a central element in our understanding of the petition. God is effective in our midst. If holiness were the decisive element in God's nature, there would be no such effectiveness. He would remain a God distant from men. Through Jesus Christ He has however shown Himself to be a God who searches for man. He has come close to man as a man Himself. Through His Son He has become the God of men. His holiness is paired with His love, and this latter becomes the determinative motif of His actions. By love He wills to draw men to Himself. For this reason He works with His Spirit among men. Thereby He remains the Holy One. It is precisely the sending of His Son to reconcile men to Himself that shows His holiness. He reverses it in such a fashion, however, that it comes to the aid of men in their need. He draws into His holiness those men who will allow themselves to be hallowed by the death of His Son. Therefore we have permission through Jesus Christ to call upon His name. Through Him God has made His name known to men (John 17:6) and has promised them to be their God so that they can become His people. Through Jesus Christ God's name as Father has been revealed to them. He is the content of what God has done for men and of how He encounters them. They now give Him glory when they call upon Him by this name since by their use of the name Father they acknowledge Him as the God who has rescued men from their own perdition.

According to Lohmeyer, "hallow" in the context of the Our Father means *to glorify God's name*. "Father, glorify Thy name. . . . I have glorified it" (John 12:27 f.). In the preaching of Jesus, in His loving service among men, in His suffering and dying, in His resurrection and ascension God Himself was therefore at work. Jesus wanted nothing more than to glorify God's name, and as He did it, God approved of Him. Consequently the petition for the hallowing of God's name becomes serious business for the ones praying. Above all they are to act in such a way that through them the name of God does not acquire disgrace and shame. This must be said not only about their lives but also about their worship. Their worship and prayer life are so often deficient in discipline that one can no longer detect that they are praying to a holy God. There should be more respect, which in turn would express itself in sanctified life and language. The First Petition is of such gravity because according to John's Gospel the glorification of God must also become apparent in suffering. *Jesus' suffering is the fulfillment of everything that belongs to God's glory.* Thus even in the suffering of the church, in her confession to God, in her faithfulness God is glorified. Here the pagan concept of

51

honoring God is completely abandoned. Man is unable to honor God if he thinks he can do something special for Him; he can honor God only when he walks obediently the path that God walks with His own to bring them to His goal. *God does not desire to have holy things, but He would have holy people who serve Him.* No matter how necessary church equipment is, for God it remains external. We cannot glorify the name of God with beautiful church buildings or with a large number of bells or great organs. The confession of His name — that entails the total dedication of a man! The externals can at best only assist in instructing him. There exists no holy cult separate from the holy men whom God would prepare via His Spirit.

Yet we must beware lest we understand the First Petition moralistically. Christians can hallow God's name only by letting Him hallow them. They must let themselves be drawn into what God Himself does for hallowing His name. They are able to glorify God's name because through Jesus Christ they are hallowed. Jesus hallowed Himself for them, and through faith they have a share in Jesus' act. *God hallows His name by making men His children,* giving them a new heart and granting them the power for a new life. "You were washed, you were sanctified, you were justified in the name of the Lord Jesus Christ and in the Spirit of our God" (1 Cor. 6:11). Thus God has given everything to those who believe in Him and has put into their lives what Jesus Christ has done for them. Jesus glorified God's name in them. They are now the separated ones outfitted by God with a new life. By the forgiveness of sins they are purified from evil. Something of God's holiness has been transmitted to them. Now they are able to praise God through word and deed. The new life granted by

God now becomes an act of God on men to glorify His name in the same fashion as the effective preaching of His Gospel among men. Through the renewal of their lives the Christians become "good trees." They are able to bear good fruit, which God expects from them since He Himself has deposited in them the seed for it. They do not now simply carry the name Lord in their mouth, but God's lordship becomes visible in their obedience and thus in their service (Matt. 7:16 ff.). By means of the new life God places them out in public. They are effective by their very being. Men begin to take note of them. They see their good works and glorify the Father in heaven. Thus in the hallowed life of the Christians the unbelievers learn to know the glory of God's own name and hallow it (Matt. 5:13 ff.). Where the new life has been given, there the church receives her missionary dimension. The environment comes into her field of radiation and becomes aware of what God has done. There is therefore no witness separated from life, and there is no mission that bypasses the total life of the church.

Mission has the significance of leading men to let God's name be hallowed among them. Jesus teaches His disciples to pray for the hallowing of God's name since it is constantly profaned by men. There are men who do not know the name of God although they are God's creatures. They deny that they belong to God's household, and they do not acknowledge God as their householder. They have made themselves lords in the issue of their belonging to God. Insofar as they allege to have no control over God, they also do not permit God to affect themselves. Many pray to other gods and deprive God of the honor of His name. They no longer relate their lives to the true God, do not subordinate themselves to His commandments, and thus dishonor God's name (Rom.

1:18-32). But God wills to become their God too, to have them acknowledge Him as Creator and Lord so that in His love He can redeem them. But that is possible only when the name of God is proclaimed to them. God's actions with man thus have a special goal that is already present in the First Petition. From this arise new aspects of the hallowing of His name.

Men who do not believe in God are unable to hallow God's name if He does not reveal it to them. When we speak the First Petition, we are praying that God would make His name known to all men and show His mercy to them. Thus even the First Petition becomes a mission prayer. We must allow God to place us into His revelatory process, which takes place today through messengers of Jesus who proclaim to men what God has done through Jesus for their salvation. If God's name is not proclaimed and therefore not revealed to them, neither can it be hallowed among them. God's name is hallowed when we witness of Him to men. When we engage in mission, we put ourselves at the disposal of God, who wants to have His name hallowed among men by the preaching of the Gospel.

For this reason Jesus understood the glorification of God's name *to be equated with the proclamation of His Gospel.* "I made known to them Thy name" (John 17:26). By the proclamation of the Gospel God is brought near to men so that they perceive His call and can be brought to faith by it. In this manner Jesus fulfilled His mission (John 17:4-6). This clearly states that the hallowing of God's name consists in its being proclaimed to men and as a result of the proclamation being believed.

On the basis of this intention of God Paul is commissioned to carry the name of the Lord to the heathen

(Acts 9:15). God wants to gather from among the heathen a people for His name. They belong to Him, for they are already called by His name (Acts 15:14 ff.). Here mission is founded on the First Petition. Paul received grace and apostleship to bring about the obedience of faith for the sake of His name among all the nations (Rom. 1:5). For the sake of this mercy the Gentiles will glorify God (15:9 ff.). In all these passages the hallowing, or glorifying, of God's name is equated with proclaiming and extending it. "To sanctify and to proclaim God's name are thus interchangeable here, and that is why the sanctified are above all exhorted: 'Through him then let us continually offer up a sacrifice of praise to God, that is, the fruit of lips that acknowledge his name' (Heb. 13:15), and their love is regarded as 'showing forth the name of God' (Heb. 6:10). So all Christian life begins and ends in acknowledging and praising the name of God in word and deed." (Lohmeyer, p. 65)

Thus the mission among the nations and the proclamation of the name in the congregations of Christians constitute the fundamental operation in the hallowing of God's name. By virtue of the service that is here required of Christians the First Petition is removed from every moralistic misunderstanding in terms of self-sanctification. It is removed from the sphere of pious edification. Because of God's goal contained within it, it takes on significance for the world and for mankind. It already has God's dominion over the whole creation in view. Of course God's name is also hallowed in worship. It is the fundamental action, for where authentic worship of God takes place, it results in the glorification of God's name among men. Glorification and proclamation of the name always occur in such a fashion that in his prayer the praying man places himself at God's disposal. God

Himself sets him free internally to extend His name among men. For this reason the praying congregation can properly hallow God's name only in witnessing, just as God would have His name hallowed in the church through His word.

In the First Petition Christians receive a vocation. Because of their faith they are made co-workers together with God. God incorporates them into His work and subordinates them to His goal. Just as He Himself revealed His name in Jesus Christ, so those who believe in Jesus Christ now make Him known among men. Here is where mission arises. Through the believers God continues what He began in awakening faith through the Holy Spirit.

In the hallowing of His name God does not consider only the individual soul, valuable as this is to Him. He always has His eye on all men. The First Petition does not limit itself to Christians, but *it aims at all mankind.* In it we already have a comprehensive concept of mission that can be restricted neither to foreign nor to home missions. God's concern is always for all men. Proclamation and thereby the hallowing of His name is genuine to the extent that it has its eye on all men, when the "all" of the New Testament remains determinative. If this is not the case, then the church's work of service even in the shape of foreign missions is contracted. The First Petition has worldwide perspectives, as God has established them in the sending of His Son (John 3:16). Through the proclamation of His name throughout the world, the rescue of all men, and the founding and gathering of His church in a world of unbelief the world again becomes God's world. The goal is one holy God in a world and a humanity that He has hallowed. In mission He shows Himself by the proclamation of His name to be the Housefather who cares, who releases nothing and no one from His household, not even when men want to escape His activity. His Father name stands over all, and thereby the world rests beneath God's love and mercy.

When God's church on earth prays the First Petition, she is unable in this single sentence to express its implied greatness. She should know, however, that this petition in God's ears contains all that He has put into it by His revelation. By this petition she is also able to be taken into the movement that proceeds from Him for the hallowing of His name. Through His Spirit she is able to become one holy people proclaiming the works of Him who has called them out of darkness (thus out of their ignorance of His name) into His marvelous light (1 Peter 2:9). Thereby she becomes a church that is on the move together with God for the salvation of men. She will be discouraged by the fact that in her earthly form she herself profanes God's name time and time again. She is nevertheless granted to know that despite all weaknesses she lives in the grand eschatological event that began with Jesus Christ and will find its completion with the coming of Jesus. (Phil. 1:10)

Thus the First Petition already designates the thought content of the Our Father. It is an explicit mission prayer. The subsequent petitions only serve to develop further what is already contained in the first.

Thy Kingdom Come

The name of God is hallowed when God's kingdom comes to men and when God sets up a new order by taking possession of men. Men profane the name of God by setting themselves outside this order through their sin. God's name is hallowed when they are led back into the kingdom of God under God's lordship. When we pray, "Thy kingdom come," we become involved in the battle that God is waging against the kingdom of sin. In prayer we confront this other kingdom.

We Christians usually forget or refuse to recognize any longer that God establishes His kingdom in a world that is already the kingdom of someone else, namely, the prince of this world. For believers this is a concrete reality since they see its consequences every day and have confirmed what Holy Scripture says about it. If there were no such other kingdom, the kingdom of God would not have to come and the proclamation of the kingdom would be senseless. Then even today everything would be encompassed under God. Everything would be subject to Him. But this is not the case since there actually are powers inimical to God. The Gospel with its message of God's kingdom can be understood only vis-à-vis the other kingdom, which Jesus Christ certainly has already conquered but which will be abolished only by the coming of God's kingdom to men. This other kingdom excludes men from the kingdom of God (Eph. 5:5). Proclaiming the name and thus also the kingdom of God presses toward the goal of overcoming the other kingdom and destroying the power of the devil. Since it has to do with overcoming the other kingdom, we Christians cannot occupy a neutral position. Neither, therefore, can we pray the Our Father as impartial observers. *We always become involved in the fight.* Thus it is part of a Christian's sense of reality that he knows the actuality and the power of the other kingdom. Only in this way does his prayer attain its rightful content. Praying for the coming of God's kingdom is always praying against the other kingdom and against God's adversary. Every petition of the Our Father is a decision for the lordship of God and thus a participation in the battle. Even if we cannot understand this "dualism," it is nevertheless there. The conflict between the two kingdoms is the thread that runs through the entire Bible.

This makes somewhat more understandable the fact that God always brings His kingdom against the opposition of those who live under the other kingdom and have therefore withdrawn from under God's commandments and His lordship. They must be freed from the spell of this kingdom and returned to God's order. Neither is the Christian community immune to the temptations of the other kingdom. That is why the petition for the coming of God's kingdom has such great urgency even for Christians themselves. We can understand why Gregory of Nyssa passed on to us the Second Petition in this fashion: "Thy Holy Spirit come and cleanse us!" The other kingdom not only brings temptation and trial to the Christian community; it also sends out the very men who want to destroy the kingdom of God. Having decided against God, they take up the fight against whatever is visible of His kingdom on earth. Through them the Christian community is put to the test and called to battle. It is always its very existence that is at stake.

That is why God fights the battle in such a way that He is very personally involved. To begin with, He has delivered us from the dominion of darkness and transferred us to the kingdom of His beloved Son (Col. 1:13). In the conflict that then arises the prayer for the coming of the kingdom is a special means of battle (Acts 4:29 ff.). There are instances in Scripture where the enmity of the other kingdom is, as it were, prayed to death. Through prayer the emissaries of God's kingdom are delivered from the enemies of God's Word (2 Thess. 3:2). God answers the prayer for the coming of His kingdom in such a way that He also proves Himself to be the Lord over the other kingdom. If this were not true, our prayer and even the battle itself would be senseless.

How little we see the reality of this battle and thus even of the kingdom of God is evident from our usual interpretation of the Second Petition as meaning that the kingdom of God is something purely in the future and not in the present. *The Holy Scriptures, however, view both the present and the future salvation, the kingdom of God in its present concealment and in its eschatological revelation, in one unbroken connection that cannot be undone.* Thus we cannot transfer its realization into the future. It is surely true that everything God does for us has an eschatological reference; but by overemphasizing the eschatological definition we run the danger of no longer laying any emphasis on the present, the *hic et nunc*. We can, however, grasp the future properly, talk about it, and pray for it only because the present nature of salvation has been revealed to us. Jesus is the Content, the Bringer, the Proclaimer, and the Completion of the kingdom. We know about His second coming only because He once came, and we can believe in Him who came only because He will come again.

The kingdom of God has come with Jesus Christ. It is here. It is now. It is a kingdom for all men, for Jews as well as for Greeks, namely, for pagans. Within it God's promises have been fulfilled. Through the proclamation of the kingdom that has come men have the opportunity to believe in the Bringer of the kingdom. With Him the eschatological event among the nations has begun. He has gathered to Himself a community subject to His will and proclaiming His kingdom (Rev. 5:9). The kingdom is here, but it will not be evident in its fullness until His second coming. Through Jesus, therefore, the kingdom of God has come; and through Him it remains a coming, eschatological subject for eternal hope. He is the Content of the kingdom, and thus it is present. He is the Bringer of the kingdom, to whom the Father has given all things; thus His kingdom is still coming, and we should pray for it. It is the same for the kingdom as it is for the name of God. There are men to whom it has come through the proclamation, and there are others who have not yet heard about it.

The kingdom of God is God's new order, which began with Jesus' coming on earth and which He makes a reality in His church among sinful mankind. It is the new relationship with God that has arisen by the death of Jesus and through the forgiveness of sins. It is the kingdom of faith that is here among men through trust in the Father. It is the order of love toward men, which He has founded in the church as the basic structure of human society. Empowered by Him, men can now meet one another in the love with which He has loved them. It is a kingdom of truth. In His Son we have been given our only Redeemer. Thereby He frees men from the kingdom of lies, from their own self-seeking and self-adulation. It is a kingdom of righteousness among men, for in the forgiveness of sins He has granted us His righteousness. Thus the unrighteousness of the other kingdom has been banned from His church. It is a kingdom of peace, for we have received His peace, which rules hearts and minds. It is a kingdom of life because He is a God of the living and the source of life. And yet the dead are nestled in His hand because He has overcome death and will call them to life. It is also a kingdom of hope, for it promises us the eternal kingdom when all restrictions that now prevent life in Him from developing will be removed. It is a kingdom of the forgiveness of sins, whereby His judgment has lost its threatening character. These are all gifts of the kingdom of God to us, which may shine even now in our earthly life. Through them His name is hallowed and His kingdom comes to men (Matt. 6:33; Rom. 14:17). These are all facts. The kingdom of God is not a dream. It does not consist in thoughts but in the effective working of God among us.

Through these gifts of God, through His activity among men, and through God's new order in the church the kingdom of God to come becomes a historical event among men. The breaking forth of the kingdom of God, as it takes place through the proclamation of His Gospel, the Gospel of the kingdom (Matt. 24:14), makes a visible incision into the history of men, which is described in the Epistle to the Ephesians with the contrast of "once" and "now." When Jesus Christ comes to men, something new begins. He raises the banners of the kingdom. Since with Jesus Christ the kingdom has entered history, it can no longer be stricken from history. Since the kingdom of God has come in Him, since it comes now through the proclamation to men, and since its fulfillment will bring the age to an end, the whole course of history is determined by the kingdom of God. *Under the kingdom all time becomes God's time.* Now we can no longer think of history apart from God. From the time of Jesus' work, death, and resurrection God has ruled the world within the coming of His kingdom and gives the world a goal. These statements will remain valid even when men do not acknowledge this kingdom but fight it and threaten to destroy it. In the last analysis their reactions can only confirm the reality of the kingdom. Sin and the weakness and failure of the church can only darken the kingdom of God on earth but never do away with it. Even in the worst events in history it is there because it is precisely where the kingdom of darkness operates in its power that the gifts of the kingdom of God shine most brightly. That is why Christians need not despair or lose confidence in God. They walk their way in the power of His kingdom.

When we pray for the coming of God's kingdom, we are asking that it may become a reality among men time and again, especially where the message of the kingdom has not yet sounded. God's lordship is all-encompassing, and thus all men are already included in it whether they know it or not and whether they want it or refuse it. That is why He can also let His kingdom come to all men. God will not allow Himself to be made a private God. He is the Lord of all men. Therefore He let His Son die for all men, and therefore through Him He has intended His kingdom to be for all men. The whole world is His; in it He sows the seed of His kingdom, the Word of God. To this end He sends His emissaries into all the world to proclaim the message of salvation to all men. Today He still calls to men: "Repent, for the kingdom of God is at hand!" Through His Word He sets up the connection between Himself and men. His Son will rule as king in His church, and through the church He will overcome everything that opposes His kingdom (Matt. 28:19). But He does not reign with force like a wordly ruler. His kingdom always remains an offer of the gifts described above, which overcome evil. The effectiveness of His power lies in the new creation, in the renewal of hearts. Therewith God sets out on a long and weary road. But He will realize the goal. The time will come when everything will be subject to Him (Eph. 2:19-21). Then He will be worshiped by all men as the only Lord.

Since God does not rule with force, His kingdom can be understood only as a gift. He forces it upon no one. No one is compelled to enter. The idea of His making it a gift is to have the receiver stretch out his hand toward it and let God give it to him. "Inherit the kingdom prepared for you" (Matt. 25:34). Since God alone controls the kingdom and with it the gift, it must be asked for. No one can appropriate it for himself. God remains the Lord of the gift since He is responsible for its efficacy and its bestowal. Since the kingdom has come with His Son, God has made Him to be the kingdom's gift to men. The kingdom of God comes only to those who are prepared to receive the Son.

The kingdom relationship consists in men letting God make them His property; then they will also "live under Him in His kingdom." To be fitted into God's kingdom means subordinating ourselves to Him as the one Lord. Luther has classically formulated this in his exposition of the Second Article of the Creed: "That I may be His own and live under Him in His kingdom and serve Him in everlasting righteousness, innocence, and blessedness." It is also a part of the kingdom relationship that we acknowledge God as the Lord of the kingdom and approach Him in prayer. In the petition for the coming of the kingdom lies our acknowledgment of His gift. If we receive the gift, we are also at the disposal of the kingdom. It always comes to us in such a way that we allow God to use us for the purposes of His kingdom. As we receive we become citizens of the kingdom, standing in the service of the Lord of the kingdom. We cannot have the gift to use for our own purposes. Then it escapes us again. Instead it is actually the gift that has us at its disposal. God takes us into the kingdom's service.

We frequently say that we are called to extend the kingdom. Is that really accurate? Is it not rather that as comrades in the kingdom we are deployed at the front which God alone decides? When we pray that God's kingdom may come, we can do so only if we desire to have God fit us into the kingdom. We receive it as disciples of Jesus. As such, however, we are always called to be witnesses of the kingdom.

No man is capable of setting up God's kingdom among men no matter how hard he tries. God does not permit us to shape it according to human ideals regardless of how beneficial that might be for human life. All efforts to achieve the kingdom of God by social measures founder on man's sinfulness. It has always finally led to revealing the signs of the other kingdom. We cannot make our human ideals the goal of God's lordship without perverting the kingdom of God. It has nothing to do with external happiness. Nowhere did Jesus promise His followers happiness. Instead He showed them the path of suffering and made suffering itself the way to glorify God. He healed the sick and fed the hungry, but He did not eliminate sickness from the world nor remove hunger from the earth. He set up signs of His kingdom. He always did it in such a way that His Father, not men, would be honored by Him. It is our privilege to do the same that Jesus did. But we shall be heading down the wrong path if we make a human program out of it. Then we are no longer satisfied with the gifts of God and no longer turn to those who have a right to them. What God's kingdom is and how it becomes a reality among men is to be decided solely by the Lord of the kingdom. Here God goes the opposite way that men would take since He has made weakness the fundamental rule of His actions. Everything depends on our letting Him give us the kingdom mentality described above. Only when based on this does everything come out right.

The kingdom of God can only be extended when God's Word and will are proclaimed among men so that the action of His Spirit makes the new creation arise among them. God has made the Gospel of Jesus Christ the message of His kingdom to be proclaimed to all. *For this reason the kingdom of God comes by extending His Word to men.* Since they cannot worship and hallow God's name unless it is proclaimed to them, neither can they come into His kingdom and serve Him if it does not come to them through the kingdom message.

In His preaching Jesus consciously latches on to the message of John the Baptist: "The kingdom of heaven is at hand." This is eternity entering time. Jesus also commissions His disciples with the message of the kingdom (Luke 9:2). They are called from the point of view of conformity to the kingdom. Anyone unwilling to be fit into the inner structure of the kingdom is rejected (Luke 9:57 ff.). He cannot use men who consider their own affairs to be more important than God's kingdom. He does not want to have any functionaries of Word and sacrament. His emissaries represent the Lord of the kingdom, and through Him they are themselves the kingdom. "The good seed means the sons of the kingdom" (Matt. 13:38). They are themselves sown so that the kingdom might spring up. They are drawn into death so that fruit can grow from their dying. In this manner Jesus Himself proclaims the kingdom and brings men redemption. Thus suffering becomes the working principle of the kingdom. In this fashion the kingdom of God came to men through Jesus and through His apostles (Mark 4:2-32). So it will continue until His proclamation has reached the ends of the earth (Acts 1:8) and the end of time (Matt. 28:20). The message of the kingdom is thus a universal message; it has a universal kingship to proclaim.

With the coming of Jesus and the breaking forth of the kingdom something decisive happened. Jesus expanded God's kingship, previously restricted to Israel, to all mankind. Now the kingdom of God is to be proclaimed as a testimony to all nations (Matt. 24:14). Thereby it becomes God's offer of grace to all men. The message of the kingdom arraigns men before God for an ultimate decision. Only when men have heard the offer of salvation will the end come — and that means not only the judgment but also the completion of the kingdom. God has made the establishment of His kingdom in glory dependent on the missionary obedience of His people. This does not imply that all men allow God to bring them into His kingdom. It only says that the church is to continue offering grace so long as God's patience requires this service. It is the great task of the church to carry out kingdom preaching among the nations and to be herself the vanguard of that kingdom. Consequently we Christians can pray the Second Petition only if we allow ourselves to be placed into service.

"All this is simply to say: 'Dear Father, we pray Thee, give us thy Word, that the Gospel may be sincerely preached throughout the world and that it may be received by faith and may work and live in us. So we pray that thy kingdom may prevail among us through the Word and the power of the Holy Spirit, that the devil's kingdom may be overthrown and he may have no right or power over us, until finally the devil's kingdom shall be utterly destroyed and sin, death, and hell exterminated, and that we may live forever in perfect righteousness and blessedness.'" (Large Catechism, Tappert, p. 427)

The kingdom of God is serious business. It is granted us as a gift. We do not have it as a permanent, assured possession under our own management. We always carry within ourselves the weakness to fall prey to the other kingdom. The New Testament speaks most sharply about such behavior of men who think they are representing the kingdom of God and yet can practice within it the morals of the other kingdom (Matt. 8:12). Our share in the kingdom of God is diminished in the measure that we think we can treat it according to our own wishes. The New Testament, however, speaks of the goal and the inheritance of Christians with great joy and with such exuberant words that we hardly dare repeat them. We can pray for the coming of the kingdom only in such fashion that we always look to Him who in the lowliness of a man brought it to us. Yet we can retain and proclaim it in faith only by speaking of the Lord, who will come to fulfill all the promises of God.

Thy Will Be Done

This petition is the logical continuation of the second. When we pray for the coming of God's kingdom, we acknowledge Him as its Lord. We recognize that in His kingdom He alone decides. But the Lord of the kingdom is no imaginary Lord. He has His will, and in addition to this He has a goal within whose confines the kingdom is realized.

The trouble with men is that they have their own will confronting the will of God. They delude themselves into thinking that their freedom and happiness lie in realizing their own will. It is the tragedy of man that he thinks the will of God questions his own existence and so he reacts to the claim of God with self-assertion. Christians act similarly when they misinterpret the freedom of God's children so as to confirm their own freedom. They do not notice that when they assert themselves and protect their own freedom they are falling for a different will. Just as there is another kingdom besides the kingdom of God, so there is also an alien will within it besides the will of God. Man in his self-assertion becomes a rebel against God and a danger to his fellowmen. When God takes us into His kingdom, He frees us from the will of the other kingdom. He frees us for His service. There is no greater freedom than to be allowed to serve God. This is also a gift of grace. Thus genuine freedom arises only insofar as we are prepared to let God bind ourselves to Him. The will of God does not eliminate our freedom. It gives it a new content and thereby helps it become fully developed. Knowing that there is a will of God gives us the freedom of decision. Through this knowledge God places us into fellowship with the citizens of the kingdom, whose community life is not disturbed by the self-assertion of individual members. If man lives by his own arbitrary will, no fellowship can be created. A community can prosper only when all members live according to the same principles and are united by one goal. Their rules of life must always point to Him who brought them together.

Thus we see that the happiness which men seek is relative. What one understands by happiness always depends on the motives shaping his wishes and the road he takes to achieve happiness. It is always a man's faith and the principles that arise from it which determine what happiness is. Man must therefore become free from himself before he can rise above things. His trouble lies in the delusion that the carrying out of his own will brings him freedom and happiness. He can become free from himself only when he adapts himself to the divine order, when he lets God make him free. Liberation from the bonds of the other will, however, is a process of faith. God takes a man into His kingdom through Jesus Christ, placing him under His order. He reveals His will to man, and man acknowledges this will as obligatory.

The will of God is always what God wills. In His Word He always speaks to men so as to reveal Himself as the Lord. God has let us know what we should do. But the revealed will of God can be understood variously. The commandments of God, which always contradict us but never the Gospel, can be interpreted very legalistically so that they no longer seem to be God's gifts to men. But the Gospel can also be misinterpreted as if there were no longer any divine commands for faith. The Third Petition calls us neither to legalism nor to indolence and arbitrariness but rather to the gracious order of God's kingdom. This constitutes the goals which God has with men. God wills to rescue men and lead them into His eternal kingdom. Even the commandments of God must be understood in the light of these goals. They give the commandments their meaning. They are not simply commandments for ordering human society, but insofar as men obey the commandments of God He takes them into the operational sphere of His kingdom. He leads them to the goal of redemption. Thus the revealed will of God becomes a gift to men. We do not pray that we may be allowed to fulfill His commandments and thus also His will, but we pray that He would let us know His will and that He Himself would carry it out. The will of God is not a naked demand asserted apart from any context, but it is God's gracious activity toward us. The petition, "Thy will be done," requires that we look not at ourselves but rather toward God, who fulfills His own will.

Therefore in this petition we are praying for three things. First, *that the will of God be done in us.* This means not only that we willingly learn to submit ourselves to God's guidance without quarreling but also that we learn to love Him for the very reason that He personally leads us and reveals His guiding hand in us.

God's will toward us becomes evident also in the great historical events that we share with our church, with our nation, and in missions with those among whom we work. We are always incorporated into world events. When God ceases to bear us up thereby, He does not do it to discourage us. We are to exemplify His grace and His judgment among men. By pulling us through, God proves that His will is glorious among men.

In the Third Petition we pray also that *God's will be done for us*. This "for us" cannot be understood except in reference to Jesus Christ, since in Him God acted for us once and for all. Since then God's every action toward us has been permeated and surrounded by His one will that was done on Calvary. With Him ultimately everything is subordinated to the goal of our redemption, even when, for example, He acts for us in trouble and danger. The "for us" means that no matter what happens to us, He is always at our side if we adapt ourselves to His will. Thus in His action toward us we can also see His answering of our prayers and therewith His help. In His guidance He Himself intercedes for us.

God's will is done in us and for us, finally, *so that He can do something through us*. When He does something in us and for us, He prepares us for His work. When He lets His will be done through us, He gives us tasks that we are to fulfill among men in this world. Our service should then reveal that God is at work fulfilling His will. When God does His will through us, He still has in mind the goal with men mentioned above. Through the commission to do His will God makes us His co-workers. He always operates among men in such a way that His own people become willing to appear as visible witnesses in His place. Thus in these three ways the will of God becomes a gift of His love to us.

71

By our prayer for the fulfillment of God's will in these three ways we are incorporating ourselves into the doing of His will. If His will can be described as the order of His kingdom, its fulfillment can be described as the characteristic of the kingdom's citizens. Those who do the will of the Father in heaven are those who belong to the kingdom of heaven (Matt. 7:21). Confessing God is always accomplished by obeying God (Luke 7:8). God has therefore not hidden His will from us. He has revealed Himself. Membership in the kingdom of God makes it possible to know and do His will because God Himself lets His will be done in His kingdom.

Thus also in the Third Petition we must understand God as the Lord over all. He is the Lord of heaven and earth, that is, there is nothing outside the sphere of His will. If His will is to be done on earth as it is in heaven, these concepts refer to the whole world, or in more modern terms, the whole universe. For God to give His Son power over heaven and earth if He Himself did not have this power would be empty words (Matt. 28:18). His power is immeasurable; hence even the smallest things are under His almighty power. There is nothing over which He is not Lord and which He could not control (Matt. 10:29 f.). But this does not mean that He makes His will valid everywhere. He allows much that is not in His will. With many things He shows great patience. This is not a sign of His weakness but of His lordship. Only He who is truly Lord can also allow His vis-à-vis freedom of action. Thus we should not immediately attribute to God's will what men have caused nor label it fate or providence. Nor is the eternal law written in the stars. Holy Scripture is full of examples showing how God's expression of His will is an answer to men's behavior. God surely has a firm goal to which He leads everything. But He does not act according to a fixed schedule. He is not an eternal law nor a governing principle; He is a living God.

This distinguishes the Christian concept of God from that of other religions. In Islam the will of God is unchangeable, set from eternity. There are no problems there. It is accomplished in every case no matter what men do. God is understood in the sense of determinism. In the Indian religions there are only eternal laws to which men's lives are subject, with no god able to change them. By contrast the Father of Jesus Christ stands in living contact with a "you." He is the vis-à-vis of man, whom He wishes to rescue. Thus the performance of His will depends on whether men subordinate themselves to God's goal and let Him operate on them. He has not eliminated men's freedom. If God's will could never be contradicted, we would not have to pray for its realization; such a prayer would be nothing but senseless words. But there is indeed another will that opposes God. It expresses itself in men by the power of sin, and it must be overcome by God. God cannot act according to a schedule, but He must so answer what men do that He may reach the goal of His kingdom.

This living performance of God's will is indicated in our petition by assuming that God's will is done in heaven (Matt. 18:10). The heavenly kingdom, where He gathers the perfected ones, conforms to His will. In contrast, men since the Fall question the will of God. They withdraw from it and act in opposition to it. That is why we pray that the will of God may be done on earth as well. That the will of God may be accomplished in His whole creation is an eschatological goal. (Eph. 1:10)

When we pray, "Thy will be done," we are thereby acknowledging the will of God. This petition includes the knowledge and the confession that God's will is not done everywhere and through every man on earth. *Thus this prayer is already accomplishing the will of God.* We can truly pray this petition only when we want to have ourselves set free from our own will. We pray it contrary to our own wishes, our self-assertion, our aspirations for power, and our pursuit of happiness. Whoever takes the petition seriously steps back behind God and leaves everything to Him. He does not stand in God's way. Thus in this prayer we already see our surrender to God.

When a man submits himself through this prayer to the goal of God, it is not a passive subjection waiting for God to act. The prayer itself is already the greatest activity. In it man tries to recognize God's will and to unite himself with it. God does not carry out His will by itself, but He makes servants out of men. Holy Scripture describes our new relationship with God in the language of conformity. Through Baptism men are united with Christ (Rom. 6:4 ff.). The old man is put to death, and the new man arises, who as God's new creation also stands within His will. We are made to conform to Jesus Christ. Thus on the basis of the new life, doing the will of God is a gift to us. The will of God is done through us in the power of Him who fulfilled it for us on the cross. Associated with Him we can bear the fruit that God expects from us. Where this fruit grows, He who has done the will of God for us is also at work (John 15:4). God's will is done on earth in association with Jesus Christ.

Jesus is the standard for all who believe in Him. His relationship to the Father was unique in that He did the will of God. He did not simply tolerate it or bear it, but He Himself stood up for God's will. He renounced doing anything of Himself. He knew He was acting on commission (John 5:30). For Him the will of God included not only God's commandments but also the love revealed in Himself and thus also the calling of men to eternal life (John 6:38 ff.). As man lives by bread, so Jesus lived by doing the will of God. That was His food. What He saw the Father do was for Him a necessity, a basic element of life. Outside this will there was no life for Him. Just as bread nourishes and keeps a man alive, so obedience to God strengthens the Christian. He is never weakened, as from hard work, but rather encouraged and strengthened by Him who does the will of the Father in him and through him. *The will of God always gives the strength for doing it.* We rightly lay a heavy emphasis on faith, but is it not part of true faith in God to know that He wants to accomplish His will through us? We are very careful in using the concept of obedience because it can lead to misunderstanding redemption by grace alone. But is there a faith that does not express itself in love and thereby also in obedience? Do we not destroy the believer's power to believe when we too strongly dogmatize grace and thus take away the joy that is always evident when God carries out His will in us and through us? We say again, the fulfilling of God's will is also a gift to us! In prayer there is no neutral ground for observers. The praying man always participates in what he prays God for. God grants His salvation to men in such a way that He converts His glorious gifts into obligations; thus the gifts are realized in the task, and the prayer is answered.

This double activity of God is a characteristic of discipleship under Jesus. Whoever does the will of God belongs to Jesus. The doing of the will of God confirms in him what God has revealed through Jesus Christ (John 7:17). The Christian faith is not simply trust in what God has accomplished for men. Nor, therefore, does it search for a foundation solely in intellectual understanding. In obedience to God the believer may gain experiences that are equally valid with intellectual insights. In the relationship with God there is a second way to achieve knowledge, namely, the "experiment" of faith, which consists in man's finding the truth of God's revelation confirmed in his own obedience toward God. He must risk something to find it out. Continuing in God's Word consists in doing the will of God. Thereby man receives the gift of knowing the truth and being made free from his own bonds (John 8:31 f.). Thus there are other ways of ascertaining truth than the way of critical judgment and deductive logic, which our theologians consider the only way. Whoever would know and do the will of God must in some cases even risk something against his better judgment so that in the particualr situation he can understand the activity of God. In Holy Scripture promise and task always stand together. We cannot have promise alone. We must always take the task upon ourselves as well. God has so ordered things that the promise is always fulfilled when the task is undertaken.

That is why giving ourselves over to the will of God also results in a certainty in prayer that surprises especially the pagans. Christians know that God grants their prayers when they conform to the will of God. Usually, however, He does not answer with a miracle, though they often ask God for miracles. He usually grants them by making the petitioner himself an instrument of the granting. God gives him a task through whose accomplishment He also grants what the petitioner really needs. Granting, therefore, is not always confirming what God has been asked to do. God's will does not always correspond to our wishes and cares. Often He even goes against the course of things as the world or His enemy has set them in motion. Nor does He always agree with great church programs, no matter how well meant. If God is to attain His goal, He must often act differently from the way we in our cleverness expect Him to act. The most remarkable thing is that when we really think over the will of God and let ourselves be drawn onto His path, we always find the best solution for our situation as well.

The prayer, "Thy will be done," also tears us away from the anxiety of life. It makes us free from the cares of life for doing His will. It incorporates us into the greatness of God's actions, into the encompassing sphere of His will. God's will is always directed toward the whole world, the total humanity. The mission emphasis of the prayer underscores this. *Through redemption God desires to bring His whole creation home to Himself.* He makes Himself both Savior and Rescuer of all men (1 Tim. 4:10). He wills that all men be saved (2:4). It is not His will that one of the little ones should perish (Matt. 18:14). God's love to men underscores and actualizes His will. His Son came to seek and to save that which was lost (Matt. 18:11). He passed on to His church God's commission for the rescue of men so that the saving message might be proclaimed to all. (Matt. 28:19 ff.)

This saving will of God is the ruling theme of the entire Holy Scriptures. We simply cannot understand how the Christian church dares pray the Our Father without being guided by this saving passion of God. For instance, for hundreds of years she has left foreign missions, which carry out the special will of God, to the discretion of individuals, with no awareness that she has thereby been documenting her own disobedience toward God. Protestant churches generally base their theology on Paul; but with what right when they do not think over

77

the mystery of the will of God? Paul gave much thought to heathen missions. He said that the mystery of God's will, which had been revealed to him, was the proclamation of the Gospel to the heathen, in other words, missions, the acceptance of pagans into God's church. On the basis of Holy Scripture this is no longer a hidden but a revealed will, one which has been delivered to the church.

Another thing that Paul had to designate a mystery — that the pagans are fellow heirs, members of the same body, and partakers of the promise in Christ Jesus through the Gospel (Eph. 3:6) — is also now revealed. That is why Paul can describe the mission to the heathen as the meaning of history and thus also the basis and the goal of God's rule among the nations. To him God entrusted His decree for the church that he might make the Word of God fully known, the mystery hidden for ages and generations but now made manifest to His saints. To them God chose to make known how great among the Gentiles are the riches of the glory of this mystery (Col. 1:25-27). It is the mystery of a history that will come to an end in the eschatological completion of the church, when through Jesus Christ heaven and earth will be brought together so that God's creation may again belong to Him alone.

This mystery of the will of God is included in our prayer. As the church of God we are incorporated into His goal in a special manner, and we should serve Him in such a way that all men may be led back to God. "The message must be proclaimed in all the world so that men may know their true Lord, join in the confession, and bow before Him in thankful praise (Rom. 10:14-18; 15:7-13)." (Hahn, p. 85.) On the basis of this knowledge Paul can describe himself as the apostle of Christ Jesus by the will of God (1 Cor. 1:1; 2 Cor. 1:1; Eph. 1:1; Col. 1:1). He did not choose his job himself, but God called him to it and laid on him, even forced on him, the mission task just as He had to do with His church again and again. There would have been no apostle Paul if the salvation of all men had not been God's will. Paul recognized the necessity of this will so strongly that he stood under an inner compulsion and feared God's judgment if he did not obey. He could not boast of preaching the Gospel; he had to do it. Woe to him if he did not do it! (1 Cor. 9:16). Where in our churches do we detect something of this inner compulsion toward missions to the heathen? It is surely present in many of the church's members, and therefore mission work is done. But it does not determine the total life of the church.

How little we in all of evangelical Christianity seriously consider the divine necessity is also evident in that we let our mission work be determined by external circumstances. When difficulties and suffering appear, then the will of God is usually no longer determinative for us. We pull our missionaries back since apparently there are no more possibilities for proclamation. But especially in mission we should know that we must be prepared to carry out the special will of God, even letting it do its work in us so that the power of the Gospel can be visualized in and through us. Do we still recognize that by carrying out the will of God we are to destroy the will of the other kingdom? Our behavior in trouble and difficulties often speaks louder than our proclamation of the Gospel in normal times.

"For where God's Word is preached, accepted or believed, and bears fruit, there the blessed holy cross will not be far away. Let nobody think that he will have peace; he must sacrifice all he has on earth — possessions, honor, house and home, wife and children, body and life. . . . Thy will be done, dear Father, and not the will of the devil or of our enemies, nor of those who would persecute and suppress thy holy Word or prevent thy kingdom from coming; and grant that whatever we must suffer on its account, we may patiently bear and overcome, so that our poor flesh may not yield or fall away through weakness or indolence." (Large Catechism, Tappert, p. 429)

How can we truly pray for God's will to be done if we constantly limit it to fit our measurements? Do we not realize that when we measure God by our own life we are questioning His greatness and the universality of His love? Should we not rejoice that God wants to accomplish His will among men through us even if it means going through suffering?

On the basis of this interpretation prayer is always a question directed to our faith. What we have said about the will of God can be understood only from the viewpoint of faith, a faith that does not doubt God's word, His promises, or His goals. It is a faith that holds with the highest conviction that man is lost before God and can be rescued only through the saving message of the cross by faith in the forgiving love of God. This love must have an inner grasp on the one who prays. He must be bothered by it. When he prays with this trust in God and with God's goal in mind, the Third Petition is not empty words. The praying man is incorporated into the activity of God, who works in His believers the will and the doing and thereby lets His will be done (Phil. 2:13). He equips His men for mission and takes them into His service. Their sufficiency is from God (2 Cor. 3:5). Thus the prayer is not a pious exercise but a world-shaping reality.

In this connection there is one last thing our petition discloses to us. When in our prayer we acknowledge God as the Lord to whom the whole world belongs, as the Housefather who cares for His whole household, we are not limiting the will of God to Christendom or to the Christian world. We are then praying that the will of God may be done everywhere, also among the pagans. This is all the more important in respect to mission work because this work must have full view of the entire unredeemed world and because it is today being carried out among all nations. *He who prays the Our Father should always have the world map before his eyes!*

5. The Action of God in the Our Father

Although the first part of the Our Father already contains everything for which we pray in the second, yet the second part is not simply a repetition of the first. Whereas the first part has to do with God's goal and God's immediate action, the second has to do with the incorporating of the church of God into this action. Whereas the first part deals with the mission of God, the mission as God's immediate work among men, the second describes the action of God in His church for enabling her to carry the Gospel farther. In this second part Jesus gives her the opportunity to bring before God all the troubles that hinder her in her service. A church that submits herself with a loving and believing heart to the first part of the Our Father will be thankful for the second part, which tells her that she may ask of God everything she needs for submitting herself to the first three petitions. God's action toward her is one of help. She is not left alone in her service. He helps her and puts in order whatever becomes a tribulation to her in her work. Thus she may ascribe everything in her life to God.

Give Us This Day Our Daily Bread

Following the great and momentous petitions of the first part, the second begins with the modest request for a livelihood, for the securities of human existence. The Gospel reveals to us the God who turns His face toward the world and toward men, the God who wills to fulfill the tasks of His kingdom in the earthly reality of human weakness. Holy Scripture does not speak ecstatically but treats soberly the concrete things without which the disciples of Jesus cannot perform their service. God acknowledges these things; He uses them in fulfilling His will.

If God's lordship extends over everything, then it is quite understandable that the name of God, the kingdom of God, and the will of God are near to us even in the things of daily life and closely related to them. What we usually try to distinguish as two sectors of God's activity — two realms or kingdoms — to achieve some clarity about God's will have basically much to do with each other. God's will is not divided but is the same for both sectors even though the method of accomplishment may be different. When the Christian believes that in one sector he is clearly bound to God's statements and that in the other he has freedom of judgment, he deludes himself greatly, for even matters of judgment can be decided only in such a way that their solution is determined by the new life God has granted. That is why God and our human existence, God and our vocation, God and our money, God and our government, God and our politics have much to do with one another.

There is no portion of life no matter how "profane" or "secular" in which man can manage by himself without God, in which God does not intervene by showing His will. Everything that concerns us in the so-called worldly realm, described here as daily bread, also belongs under the category of hallowing His name, which we pray for while living in this very world. The petition for daily bread is a recognition of the Giver of all good gifts; giving thanks for it is a glorification of God. Properly administering these gifts, which is our obligation and responsibility before God, belongs under the new order of God's kingdom. Using the gifts according to His will is a recognition of His rulership.

Whereas the first three petitions deal with the goals of God, the subsequent petitions describe our sonship, our submission under the Housefather, our dependence on the Lord, our belonging to God, and our love and thankfulness toward Him. *They involve therefore the right attitude before God.* Children of God can pray only as members of the entire family. In the light of the Fourth Petition man's relationship to God can be reduced to a very simple formula: Man does not eat because he lives, but he lives because he eats. If he were lord of his life, he could also have life by his own absolute power and support it himself. He would not then be bound to God. But since his life is a gift of God, which he receives anew every day, the support of his life is also a gift of God's grace. Man lives by the goodness of the Father, who cares for him. His life would cease if God did not present him with bread and everything else included in that concept. Man remains in the household of God. That is the foundation of his life. The behavior of the pagans disregards these basic facts of our existence.

On the basis of Holy Scripture it is self-evident that

God as the Housefather supports and cares for all His creatures. The birds in the air and the lilies of the field are not too small or worthless for Him (Matt. 6:25-34), and the cosmos with its millions of stars is not too great for Him. It is not this that we men find incomprehensible, but the simple sentence: "Are you not of more value than they?" Man is so highly esteemed in God's eyes that His care applies to him above all. God has set man apart from the other creatures and designated him the being to whom His love applies in a special manner, the member of His creation to whom He pays special attention. God is still the Father who thinks of everyone and everything, but He accepts the children of men especially. He turns especially to them because the very way He formed them means that only they sense the world-wide trouble that their existence has brought about. They suffer from anxiety of life, a result of their sin that has ruined God's world. That is why He upholds them and takes care of them day after day, because for them every night is full of the warnings of insecurity, dread, and death.

Even if today's man believes he can do away with insecurity, predict the future, and shape everything according to his own will, he can do it only by increasing his insecurity. We experience this daily with our technology. The more men learn to determine the future and to shape the world and the more they make God's world into a world of men, the more also all humanity as well as the life of every individual is made dependent on unpredictable factors the individual cannot possibly control anymore. Every new invention usually becomes the source of new insecurity. We act as though we could do away with unexplainable and unpredictable things, and our pride does not allow us to admit that we are only increasing our uncertainty. Man thereby becomes dependent on powers whose control is in the hands of only a few and whose failure endangers the lives of millions. Who will give the individual a guarantee that these few desire to do good and that they are capable of controlling things so that no damage will be done? Our insecurity does not decrease with progress; it actually increases to the same extent that we must rely on men. The more technology advances, the more man becomes a danger to himself. Is not the psalmist right when he says: "It is better to take refuge in the Lord than to put confidence in man" (Ps. 118:8)? And today we should add, "or to put confidence in technology"!

But God remains as He is. He watches over our days and our lives. He gives us daily what we need when we do our work in His service. That is why we may also lay ourselves to rest every day with thankful and hopeful hearts. We may begin each new day in His name and thus in the knowledge that it comes from Him and is protected in His hand. *God leads us through all our days.* He does not take our cares away. He has so ordered things that man has a right to make a living. We must especially emphasize this today since man has a tendency to regard work as something of a burden. We are coming gradually to the originally pagan idea that man ought to be able to get along without work. On the contrary, God has both commanded and ennobled work. He put man into the world so that he could care for his own life. He gave him the privilege to be His co-worker in the world He created. Nowhere has God given His blessing to laziness. Neither should the lazy man expect that God will grant him the Fourth Petition. God gives men work to do and lays His blessing on it. Only this knowledge gives our prayer its inner freedom.

It is not the force of technology nor the burden of trouble that is determinative for men but rather the fact that God also uses our work in giving us daily what we need. That is how He keeps us from worry. Every day, including the coming day, is in God's hand (Matt. 6:34). When we pray for daily bread and everything that goes with it, we are then praying against everything that would deny us our daily bread. Praying does not mean simply giving ourselves over to fate or adapting ourselves to the unavoidable, but the praying man is a fighting man even in the area of his daily needs.

Although a fatalistic attitude toward life dominates in all non-Christian religions in spite of a lively religious life, and insecurity continues to become a source of new religiosity, the amazing thing about God's revelation is that on the basis of our sonship it daily brings us freedom from care. This is epitomized in the Fourth Petition. Whether we pray with Luke, "Give us each day our daily bread," or according to Matthew, "Give us this day our daily bread," or according to better sources, "Give us this day our bread for the morrow," is of no importance. Each of these formulations expresses our freedom from worry and our trust in God, for each one states that God will do it till the end of our days. That is why men are also allowed to pray every day for daily bread; and those who are needy and hungry every day can live as though they had everything because they can allow themselves to be the daily recipients of gifts.

The Fourth Petition, therefore, is not necessarily a prayer in time of trouble but an expression of our status as children toward the Father. Of course in time of need we can pray it with particular emphasis because in the word "daily" God also promises to grant it. It is unimportant whether we include in daily bread everything that

Luther mentioned in the Small Catechism. Since God is Lord of all, we may pray for everything that determines our lives — for health (2 Cor. 12:8), for *every* government and not only for our own, therewith also for justice and peace (1 Tim. 2:1 f.), for our enemies (Matt. 5:44), and naturally also for all men who have become our neighbors. The prayer knows no bounds when we know that God controls everything we pray for and when we subordinate our wishes to His will.

Together with the introduction to the Our Father, the Fourth Petition places us into a great fellowship. The "us" appears here to match the "our" in the introduction. *Thus we are bound together with all believing and praying men.* The family of God stands vis-à-vis its one Lord, its Housefather. The praying church is understood as a unity; what we pray for here is necessary for everyone, and God can give it to all. Before God we are placed into one great solidarity that unites all men no matter where they are or what their social position. We acknowledge God as Lord of the great Christian fellowship. But it would be false to refer exclusively to the Christian church with that "us." We would be praying the second part of the Our Father no more rightly than the first if we did not thereby think of the entire human race, the whole household of God, which stands under His care. The "us" is surely an expression of the community of praying Christians, but it joins the praying men with all other men, who live just as much by the goodness of God. The "us" reflects the creatureliness of the whole creation to which we belong. *When we pray the Our Father, we pray as members of the whole human race.* Just as God takes care of us, so He upholds all. Just as He bears our troubles, so He would like to relieve the needs of all men. The bread which we receive is the nourishment by which the entire human society lives. Thus we dare not pray selfishly, as God's children we cannot greedily and egotistically claim bread for ourselves alone. We are always privileged to share the bread God gives us with those who do not have enough. We pray as Christians who know the one Lord willing to care for all men. We therefore pray also for the rest of mankind, for the hungry and needy who have not yet found the way to the one Father. We cannot pray the Fourth Petition without also praying that God would open their eyes to the fact that it is He who satisfies even their hearts with food and gladness (Acts 14:17). When we think of the hungry people, we learn again that even our bread is a gift of God. Through the Fourth Petition Jesus makes us into fellow creatures with the rest. That is why we Christians have been given a special responsibility to work for social justice and to bear the troubles of others (Matt. 25:34 ff.). Thereby the prayer for daily bread becomes a prayer for humanity.

On the other hand, the Fourth Petition is a genuine prayer for the church because only she knows of daily bread's ultimate connection with God. She knows God as the Giver of all good gifts. She knows the necessity of a livelihood for the service which God has given her to perform. She prays with an inner tie to God, recognizing where true responsibility lies. God, who sent His Son into this earthly world to redeem men from their sins, also gave Him the authority to help them in their extremity. Along with the proclamation of the Gospel, Jesus made His care and assistance for men characteristics of the kingdom of God. Redemption from sin is not accomplished on a purely spiritual level. When man has been set free from sin, he also attains a new attitude to the things of life, to work, and to his fellowmen. In eternity the signs of deficiency in our lives are eliminated. There is neither hunger nor thirst anymore (Rev. 7:16). This is not simply a hope to make us glad but a promise that with redemption and with the breaking forth of the new creation even men's needs already stand under the banner of redemption.

In the light of this eschatological goal Jesus has made bread into a symbol of eternal life. Just as daily bread preserves life, so the bread of heaven transmits eternal life (John 6:32 ff.). It is the bread that creates life. Through Jesus Christ the splendor of eternity lies on the bread. "And just because of this splendor, this daily bread could be used as a vehicle and parable by our dying Lord, whose body is broken like daily bread and given to us as the heavenly food that we need, just as we need the daily bread on our tables. Therefore the ancient Christians could never pray the Lord's Prayer without also thinking of this *spiritual* food." (Thielicke, p. 87)

Holy Scripture makes no sharp distinction between earthly and heavenly bread. They constitute a unity. Bread becomes a symbol that illustrates the kingdom of God. Through this bread God produces the most intimate fellowship found in the kingdom of God. The fellowship of eating together becomes a parable of the close fellowship the Lord will grant His people. All men are invited to the "eating of bread" in the kingdom of God. God will not deny His fellowship to anyone who accepts His invitation. It is also the ultimate meaning of the Lord's Supper that it can be offered to all.

Thereby the Fourth Petition points us farther than to our cares about our livelihood. It has a mission reference just as other petitions do. *In their cares about their human existence, Christians cannot step out of fellowship with men; they can only share the gifts of daily bread*

91

with them. But they may actually forget that they have a need for redemption in common with other men! (If they had understood this properly, this solidarity would never have permitted the rise of race conflicts. Then neither would the so-called Christian nations have been able to enrich themselves with the bread of other nations.) Christians have sinned precisely with the things that belong to the Fourth Petition. Wherever we are granted these insights, the Christians are today called on more so than ever before to share their bread with other men.

And yet for us Christians social assistance should not stand in the foreground. We can surely allay outward distress with such assistance, but that is not enough since the roots of this distress lie in men's sinful behavior. It can really be eliminated only when men are renewed in their hearts. But this can happen only through the Gospel. For the relief of distress, preaching the Gospel is therefore at least as important as material assistance. It is not external things that change the world, but the new way of thinking, which teaches us so to use the things of this world that no harm may come to our fellowmen. Bread symbolizes redemption; therefore it should also be a Christian's first concern to offer men the true bread of life. It is important in our work that we view body and soul together; but to the same degree it is dangerous for us to emphasize only social assistance and to describe it as God's way to men. We cannot lead men into the kingdom of God with earthly bread. But contrariwise, it is a law of the kingdom of God that to those who seek His kingdom daily bread will also be given (Matt. 6:33). Without misinterpreting the passage we can probably add: Whoever wants nothing but to proclaim to men the kingdom of God will together with the Kingdom also offer them what they need in their distress. But there is always the danger that social assistance becomes primary and the message of the kingdom of God retreats into the background.

Everywhere we can observe that when men take the message of the Kingdom seriously, their social distress also begins to abate. *When the kingdom of God determines a man's way of thinking, he also learns to administer and use properly the things God has already given him.* Misuse of God's gifts causes much distress. The misuse is eliminated to the degree that one is bound in his conscience to God. Whoever has been inwardly renewed becomes more industrious and more responsible so that he already learns to live a better life with the means at hand than he could before. That is why the proclamation of the Gospel is everywhere accompanied by social improvement. In contrast to this it is very seldom that by receiving physical help one is made to change his way of thinking, to turn to God, and to live responsibly with the gifts he has received. In fact, it is generally evident that mere social assistance increases social turmoil. It simply confirms men in their materialism.

Whoever seeks first his daily bread is always in danger of hardening his heart against the message of God's kingdom. Nor can he become a witness and an emissary of the Kingdom, because the Gospel is something secondary for him. Nor does he know anything more about the blessing of poverty or the comfort of freedom from care, both of which have great importance in the kingdom of God. Thus the frequent emphasis on external conditions for church and mission work come under critical examination. Whenever they determine the work and when the work is made dependent on them, the will of God is not being done. Poverty and riches in the light of Holy Scripture have very little to do with the extension of the Gospel. It is a matter of faith and of giving ourselves to the Gospel. What is decisive first of all is whether Christians let themselves be permeated by the spirit of Jesus Christ. Then their work becomes independent of the social situation. *The decisive thing is not material prerequisites but the inner freedom to witness.* When this is present, the external things take care of themselves. That is why no one can use his social situation as an excuse for his lack of witness. Churches and missions ought to be able to let their commission determine their external existence, not vice versa. If the work is measured by financial possibilities, God cannot then give with the commission that which the church and the mission need for carrying it out. They will not dare to undertake and to do in God's name more than what seems certain according to their human calculations. Money cannot substitute for faith; it always defeats it whenever something should be dared for God's sake. And along with faith they also lose the spirit that should permeate the work.

In our times and with our riches we should be able to see something more of the daring courage with which the Lord sent His apostles on their way. Mission can be carried out only on the basis of the task itself and in the freedom from care that is founded on trust in the Lord of the kingdom (Matt. 10:9-10). The Lord of the sending is also the Lord of the bread. He promises that the disciples who carry out His work will never lack, and afterwards they can confess that the Lord has kept His word (Luke 22:35). Jesus gives them the certainty in prayer that their provident Father knows better than they do what they need when working in His service (Matt. 6:8). Only seldom can this attitude be found nowadays in church and mission. That is why they are vulnerable to the temptations that come with money. The danger is great that we

94

sin most in our care for daily bread and all that belongs with it.

Forgive Us Our Trespasses

God is not only the Giver but above all the Forgiver. He sees to it that even in external things His household remains in good order, but it is of greater importance for Him to keep the relationship of men toward Him as well as their life together in equally good order. He does this by placing men's social communication on the foundation of forgiveness. Even this has more than spiritual meaning, for in forgiveness often lies the gift for external existence as well. Even the forgiveness of sins has a strong social reference. Since men's sins destroy their relationship to God, they are also unable to find their proper relationship to one another and to God's creation. The will of God is made powerless, and God's household is broken up. That is why it is God's primary care to create through the forgiveness of sins a new basis for men's life together, to bind them to His person, and to put them to work responsibly for Him. This all happens because He is above all the Forgiving One who draws men back to Himself.

This takes place through the proclamation of the Gospel. *Through the message of God's kingdom man recognizes his sins.* He learns to know Him for whose sake God forgives him his sins. When the message of the Kingdom is offered, man also learns that he may ask God for His most fundamental gift, the forgiveness of sins. In praying for forgiveness a man acknowledges God as Lord and Judge. He confesses the holiness of God's name. He submits himself to the order of the Kingdom and makes the will of God the standard for his actions, the critique of everything he does. He also incorporates himself into the will of God insofar as he himself forgives and prays for God's forgiveness of others. Thus the prayer for forgiveness of sins glorifies God. To understand the Our Father, it is not important whether we pray with Luke for the forgiveness of sins or with Matthew for the forgiveness of debts. In both cases the meaning is that God should not carry out His charges of guilt against us but strike them from the record. By doing this He helps men, by the forgiveness of sins, to lead a liberated life hallowed by Him.

God forgives the sins of those who ask for it and thereby Himself sets up the new order and fellowship among men. Through forgiveness He makes believers the citizens of His kingdom, giving them a child relationship to Himself. Thus He makes them what they originally were before the fall into sin. Salvation through forgiveness consists in our being allowed to live here and now in fellowship with God, which someday in the final perfection will be free from all disturbance. Through forgiveness redemption becomes a gift of God. Praying for forgiveness therefore acknowledges the redemption God has granted through men and thereby corresponds to what God did for them on the cross. The religions of self-redemption have no such prayer for forgiveness in this sense. For them sin can only be a mistake that can be corrected and made good again. Redemption exists only when God through His act of redemption has already promised to grant the prayer for forgiveness and when man no longer has to live in doubt about how he can redeem himself. He is redeemed! This is the fact of the Christian message.

Since we are always in danger of acting against God's will and falling into sin, the fellowship set up by forgiveness is no certain possession. Every day we can sin and violate the will of God. It is only through God's lasting forgiveness that we can retain the status of children. Thus forgiveness is just as necessary as daily bread. *Just as God daily gives us the necessary bread, so He also daily forgives us our sins.* Just as we pray daily for the gift of bread, so we may also pray daily for the forgiveness of our sins. Just as God preserves His creatures by providing them every day with everything necessary, so also He proves His faithfulness in spite of our sins by continually searching us out and forgiving us our sins for Jesus Christ's sake. In forgiveness we see His patience and love. When we talk about God, we can only speak of the forgiving God. We can proclaim Him only because we are the ones He has forgiven.

It is a great delusion to believe that we could work in God's service without the forgiveness of sins. We must be accepted by God before we can confess Him in our lives. We must feel something of the power of forgiveness before we dare to dedicate our lives to Him. *Forgiveness gives the impulse and the power that enable us to serve.* If church vocations today suffer from lack of men, this is partly connected with the fact that daily forgiveness of sins is no longer a reality. The failure of Christendom in mission can only be explained by this central Gospel issue. When a man receives the forgiveness of sins, he also receives the knowledge that he must pass on the Gospel of the forgiveness of sins to those who need it for their salvation. Through the unburdening of his conscience he is made free. The bonds that have held him prisoner within his own interests are broken. Forgiveness is always a liberation for service and witness. Whoever has received forgiveness cannot help passing it on to those who are still far from God.

On the basis of this fundamental prerequisite God

establishes His new order among men. Just as God takes us into His fellowship through forgiveness, so should we also share our fellowship with our fellowmen through the gift of forgiveness. Our fellowship with God should determine our relationship with others. Just as He has freed us from our own self-seeking through forgiveness, so we also should forgo our ambitious claims in the fellowship of men. He wants us to forgive men as He has forgiven us. Thus the forgiveness of sins serves to order the common life of men with one another. Only if His children practice peace and reconciliation with one another does God's household remain in order. God actually makes men's willingness to forgive one another the prerequisite of His own forgiveness. Peace with God does not exist unless we keep peace with men. We cannot have fellowship with God if we do not want to accord God's peace to our brothers and sisters. The Gospel has profound effects on human society. For this reason we dare not present the message of the Gospel in a one-sided spiritual fashion. Wherever the Gospel orientation toward men is missing, relationship with God is also unfeasible. The same applies to the life of prayer, which appears so impotent because the people who pray have not yet achieved the proper relationships with their fellowmen. Jesus designates the petition for forgiveness and the intercessors' forgiveness of one another as the prerequisite for genuine prayer and the answer to prayer (Matt. 6:14; 7:1-5). Prayer without willingness to forgive does not penetrate to the heart of God. That is why the Fifth Petition is so important within the Our Father.

It is not only by personal transgression of God's commandments and against our fellowmen that we also in our self-centeredness make ourselves guilty before our fellowmen. *Sin also includes that which our fellowmen do and to which we silently consent.* We must realize that we can commit sin in the political realm by simply accepting everything without rebuke. The sins of the so-called Christian nations, sins that have received Christianity's silent consent, have become the greatest hindrance to the extension of the Gospel. Guilt can also consist in denying our fellowmen what God has intended for them through us. Here we ought not to think only of material things. What we deny them can also include a good word, the testimony of the Gospel, the service of love to the poor and the sick. The gifts of God that we receive in terms of the first three petitions are designed for all men. We become guilty before God and men when we withhold from men the greatest thing God has prepared for them.

We can serve God only by using His gifts according to His will. This also applies to the spiritual gifts that He has bestowed on His church to equip her for her service. We usually consider them as gifts for our self-edification and thus misuse them. The servant who makes God's gift his own possession and tries to conserve it is liable to judgment (Matt. 25:14-30). He is just as bad as the Christian who knows the will of God but waits to see what others do and then makes his decision dependent on them. Is this not the point of God's actual charges of guilt against us? One often has the impression that God takes the misuse or embezzlement of His gifts much more seriously than that which we call sin. God wants to help other men through the gifts He has given His people. They do not contribute to our own sanctification unless we use them for others. By such proper use of God's gifts we mature into full manhood in Christ.

If we do not use God's gifts, we forgo the freedom to do good with them. We forfeit the means and the energy for fulfilling the divine will. God's gifts are always our equipment for His assignment. If we operate with them as though they were under our own jurisdiction, we incriminate ourselves with God and leave our debt to men unfulfilled. For this reason the petition says: "Forgive us our debts as we forgive our debtors."

What God gives the individual, He gives in such manner that the receiver can use it for others. One might almost say that if it had not been meant for others, he would not have received it. Humanly speaking there is no such thing as preference before God. Every gift is a confirmation of our call into service. This fact imparts an overwhelming significance to the pronouns "us" and "we." It is true that we have to stand before God as individuals and ask for forgiveness, but it is just as significant that we pray the Our Father as members of a fellowship that constitutes a unity before God. Our offenses against others are certainly a personal act, but by virtue of the connection between members of the church as the body of Christ they become sins that affect the whole church, as the sins of the fellowship are conversely reckoned to the individual. Therefore the petition for forgiveness places us into solidarity with our brothers and sisters. Together with them we comprise not only a fellowship of sinners but also a congregation of praying people who by the forgiveness of sins become a brotherhood of the forgiven. No fellowship can be put in order and survive if its members do not make forgiveness the basis of their common life. Through the forgiveness of sins everything is swept aside that disturbs the peace of God in the congregation. (Eph. 2:11-22)

At this point the Fifth Petition has its profound connection with the Lord's Supper. In the Supper Jesus grants His fellowship to His disciples through the forgiveness of sins and by His presence brings into existence the fellowship among the members of His body. Thus Christians mediate to one another in forgiveness what they themselves have received from their Lord. They are unable to forgive one another if they are not prepared to confess and repent of their sins (Matt. 18:21 f.). They cannot even properly ask for forgiveness if they do not look upon Him who by His suffering has become their forgiveness. Yet Jesus made forgiveness of sins the content of His saving message for all men. Since He died for all men and by His death wishes to rescue all men from destruction, the message of forgiveness leads to mission. This is the center of the message that Christians have in contrast to the other religions.

In the petition for forgiveness of sins the universal message of the Gospel becomes recognizable. The question is not put whether men wish to be redeemed in this way. The Biblical message demonstrates its origins in God also by not making redemption dependent on human volition. God redeems and offers rescue to man. Thereby the church gets a double assignment. She must pass on to men the message of redemption so that they may be able either to respond to it in faith or to refuse it. But the church can pass on the message only if she herself represents mankind. The church stands in sinful solidarity with those to whom she preaches the forgiveness of sins.

In the church the whole human race stands vis-à-vis the holy God. She pleads forgiveness for all. The "us" reminds Christians that they cannot remove themselves from the world. In the petition for forgiveness we confess our commitment not only to the holy God but also to men who know nothing of forgiveness. Thus we cannot pray the Fifth Petition without becoming united with the rest of mankind in painful consciousness of sin. We know that God preserves the world only for the sake of forgiveness. Christians perform a vicarious function, which the world may well not acknowledge but which in God's eyes is the priestly service of Christianity. God entrusts mankind to them. Christians are always participating in God's actions in the world, since in prayer they themselves exercise influence on it.

In the petition for forgiveness the Christian church presents herself before mankind and intercedes for them. As God makes man's need His own by the suffering and dying of His Son, so the cross is the sign for the church that she may place herself on the side of men so that they may be saved from the distress of their sin. The church is a fellow bearer of the world's sin in that in prayer she brings these sins before the Father who forgives them for the sake of His Son. She bears the world in the love that God has granted her.

Through the forgiveness of sins the church attains her missionary dimension. She would not dare tell men the message of Jesus Christ if she herself did not know of its power. She would have no joy for mission if she did not know by receiving the forgiveness of sins that all men could be saved by it. She is privileged to pass on what she has received to others who need it for their salvation just as much as the Christians. The significance of forgiveness for all men makes the church realize that she has been privileged by God. By preaching the forgiveness of sins the church calls the rest of mankind to conversion. With this she fights against the sins of men. Hearing this message, they forsake their sinful ways and give honor to God (Acts 2:38). Thereby the offer of forgiveness becomes the mission call, the content of the mission preaching, the proclamation of the Kingdom. Forgiveness of sins is the foundation of the mission task. In the name of Jesus repentance and forgiveness of sins should be preached to all nations (Luke 24:47). And so the church's work of mission is directly bound up with our petition.

If Christians do not undertake this task of mission, they become guilty before God and men. Since they have received the forgiveness, which belongs to the order of relationship with God, they are permitted to become instruments of God for other men. Since they have heard the message of the Gospel, they are obligated to the rest of mankind. Now they have become debtors themselves (Rom. 1:14). They possess something that is meant for all men. If they do not pass it on to them, they owe them something and become disobedient toward God. Since Christendom has seldom recognized her obligation to carry out missions, she goes along under a burden of guilt that hems in her own life because it is unrecognized and unconfessed guilt. Thus she must ask God for forgiveness for her lack of mission work. Without forgiveness of this guilt and without the renewal of her life in witness she cannot be thankful for the forgiveness of sins. Mission always begins by Christendom herself repenting for what she has neglected. When the forgiveness of sins awakens her conscience in this area once more, she will also gladly place herself in the service of the commission. The beginning of missions is never based on what men should do but on what God has done for them. When men recognize this, they also realize that God does not extend His message in miraculous ways but through men who believe in Him and who can pass on His gift. He has made mission work dependent on His church's faith and obedience. Does not the preaching of the forgiveness of sins also belong to those unused talents that He has entrusted to His church?

The forgiveness of sins in its greatness — it can never be surpassed — and in its breadth — it is promised to all men who believe in Jesus — also gives growth to the Christians' intercessory prayer. When they receive the forgiveness of sins in this depth, they also feel the inner distress of unredeemed man laid on their hearts and consciences. Thus prayer becomes the first step toward missions (Rom. 10:1). Christians find no inner peace, for they cannot bear the lost state of others. This drives them to pray that God would have mercy on them.

Thus prayer becomes the point of departure for mission work, and it remains its foundation since Christians can do nothing without God. Prayer is always possible, even when the situation appears completely hopeless. Prayer and intercession are exempt from all outside influences if those who pray stay faithful themselves. Persecution and enmity can hinder, confine, and destroy mission work. Human failure can make it fruitless. But the faithfulness of God never fails. That is why intercession and prayer are still possible even when everything seems hopeless. They are deeply determined by forgiveness, and so the praying man can himself intercede for those who hinder the course of the Gospel. Even when the man who prays must participate in the high honor of martyrdom, he may still pray for the rescue of his enemies and for their forgiveness (Acts 7:59; Luke 23:34). At this point we see that prayer is the only means of mission remaining for Christians in times of tribulation. When a man, as the one commissioned by God, can do nothing more, he may lay everything into the hands of Him

whose work often begins only when men no longer know
what to do.

This would all be nothing but empty words if the
prayer for forgiveness did not have a relation to eternity.
Just as all petitions in the Our Father are directed
toward eschatology, so here too eternal salvation and
God's final acts with men are involved. When God forgives us our sins here in time for Jesus' sake, it is not a
symbolic act but valid reality. When we forgive others
who have sinned against us, it does not have mere symbolic significance. Forgiveness always forestalls God's
sentence of judgment; it is valid eternally (John 20:23;
Matt. 16:19). It is verified by God in judgment, for God's
action in judgment is nothing other than what He has already anticipated on earth. Thus forgiveness becomes rescue from judgment, the promise of eternal salvation. In
forgiveness God joins us to the work of grace that He
alone carries out, for only He is the Lord who can acquit
sinners. This is the Word of God in which Christians participate. Their royal priesthood consists in their right to
practice grace when justice ought to be taking its course.
That is why forgiveness is the expression of God's love
to us.

Lead Us Not into Temptation

In proclaiming the message of His kingdom, God
has set up a goal for men. The way to it is the forgiveness of sins. But translating men into the kingdom of His
dear Son does not mean that the believers are taken out
of the world. God keeps them in the world so that
through their very presence God's activity in them can be
visible before the world.

Since Christians live in a world that is a daily temptation to them, they are in danger of regarding the world
more highly than the will of God. Thereby they fall back

into sin and separate themselves from God. They are not immune to temptation. Their sinful inclination makes them susceptible to seductions and temptations. Just as they have an endowment that enables them to hear God's voice, so also they have an inclination that is attuned to the prince of this world. Christians constantly face both possibilities in their decision. They can serve God or the devil. There is no middle road for them. Thus their lives often follow a line thin as a razor's edge. First of all they live in tension between good and evil, between what they should do according to God's will and what they would like to do for their own sake. Then they must be constantly deciding for or against God. Then, too, Satan wants to divert them from their goal and return them to the situation in which they were before they came to faith. Thus Christians must always stand the test. Since they often fail in this, they are in danger of forfeiting their salvation. That is why the Sixth Petition is necessary for them. They pray their Father in heaven to preserve them in the midst of temptation.

Jesus' disciples cannot escape temptation. Also in this respect they are not above their Master. *They are tempted just as their Lord was tempted* (Matt. 4:1 ff.). The basic elements of this temptation repeat themselves in the life of every Christian and in the life of the church. No matter how right it is that Jesus was tempted for us, this still does not mean that temptation can no longer touch us. Jesus' temptation is not behind us. Nor did it bring a decision for us. Temptation is always present when we place our own well-being higher than God's will, when the pursuit of our own image and influence means more to us than the Gospel's counsel for living. Like the evil foe, we too are capable of explaining away the will of God, as so many examples in our theol-

106

ogy prove. Temptation is put before us in the same way it was before Jesus. With Him too it was men — Peter, for example — who wanted to keep Him from doing the will of God. Men can also be so impressed by the things of this world that they forget their calling. All temptations appeal to men's ambition, greed, desire for power — in short, to their self-glorification. They are tempted to build a kingdom for themselves instead of serving the one kingdom. Thus we stand in constant danger of leaving the kingdom of God behind us and of losing our salvation. Jesus' own temptation shows us how to act in temptation. He grounded His decisions so thoroughly in the Word of God that the tempter forsook Him.

The petition "Lead us not into temptation" has caused distress to many a theologian. Literally it would mean that God Himself leads us into temptation, and therefore we pray that God would not do it. On the basis of the total understanding of Holy Scripture, however, the petition must not be understood as if God Himself would seduce us into sin. It is much more the case that God should stand by us in temptation and prevent us from falling prey to an alien will. "Jesus teaches His own to pray, 'Let nothing become a temptation to us,' and thus makes it clear that *everything* can become a temptation, indeed, that life itself is but one long peril and temptation" (Thielicke, p. 125). Jeremias translates it, "Let us not fall into temptation." What is important is that God always preserve us. This is confirmed in an extracanonical saying of Jesus: "No one can obtain the kingdom of heaven who has not passed through temptation." "Here it is expressly stated that no disciple of Jesus will be spared testing through temptation; it is only the overcoming of temptation that is promised the disciple" (Jeremias, p. 30). Thus God allows the testing of our faith without letting us thereby fall into the hands of alien powers. In temptation He upholds us in the position of faith. That is why the petition has only one meaning if we believe that God is stronger than ourselves and more powerful than the tempter. Hidden in God's hands we are protected from surrendering ourselves to the will inimical to God, which appears before us in seductive temptations, and from listening to the tempter's many voices in this world. Power flows into us to honor no other name than that of the heavenly Father and to serve Him alone. By praying, "Lead us not into temptation," we acknowledge God's lordship even over our enemies.

Temptation would always seduce us to stand against God. Thus it comes to us in great as well as small things. We are thinking here of the trespassing of God's commandments. If we give way to temptation, we appropriate to ourselves what belongs to God and our fellowmen. Temptation can mean that a man lets his covetousness have sway, and so he grasps after the property of another. Covetousness can lead him to break up a marriage or to sin within marriage. Then the Christian is susceptible also to the temptation of regarding his brother haughtily, of judging him, and of publicizing his sin instead of restoring him through the Word of God. But those who would be rich are tempted most of all.

Thus temptations are also connected with the concern of Christians for their lives (1 Tim. 6:9). Men are no longer satisfied with what God in His providence bestows on them, or with what He allows to grow by the labor of their hands. Temptations arise when Christians regard their own lives more highly than those of their fellowmen, when they could come to their rescue or be at their service but do not do so. It is not the ultimate temptation when they must make decisions, when they are persecuted and then, in order to save their own lives, deny the name of God and flee from suffering. The frightening thing in this is that with every temptation that they have not resisted they become weaker in their resistance. In such a case temptations appear as punishment for their sin and force them into a position in which they must sin again and again. They fall into a spell from which they cannot free themselves alone. When temptations thus achieve the upper hand, Christians fall from their child relationship with God. Their lives return to pagan ways. Neither in this petition can the praying man, therefore, separate himself from the rest of mankind. Is it not the pagans who are described in the Holy Scriptures as men who cannot resist? In our petition there is help also for them.

According to Holy Scripture, Satan sees it as his chief task to sift the church of God on earth, to place her total existence into question. He would like to destroy her power, weaken her witness, restrict her activities (Luke 22:31). He pulls individuals out of the safety of the church and seduces them into sins prevalent among the pagans. Through the sins of Christians he nullifies the church's influence on the world around her. He prevents the church from receiving a unified will determined by God. He lays oppression and persecution upon her to force her away from God (1 Thess. 3:5). He seduces her into denial and betrayal. Thereby every Christian congregation loses its missionary dimension. It can no longer be an effective example to the surrounding world.

Wherever a person has come to faith, there the tempter is also at work. A Christian would despair if he were not allowed to understand all this in its higher meaning. God has called him as co-worker in spreading the Gospel. He makes him His servant. It is in this ser-

109

vice that the fight arises. God makes him a partner in it. That is why temptations and tribulations must arise. Thus his life attains a certain meaning. In the service of God he is allowed to walk through the world in constant tribulation so that men may see how a man can prove himself in the power of God. That is why the Christian is privileged to detect God's special help precisely in temptation and to experience His unchanging faithfulness. Every temptation teaches him to look upon what he has already received from God and allows him to hope for what he especially needs in the battle. The Christian also knows that his Lord went through the same distress. Therefore he is not alone. He is privileged to sense the presence of Jesus. His Lord Himself takes up intercession for him when he can no longer pray, and He prevents the foe from achieving victory. In every weakness He strengthens his faith. In all despair He gives courage. He lays into his heart eternal hope, which makes everything earthly appear as nothing. The hour of temptation and its withstanding, therefore, is always an hour of Jesus' presence (Luke 22:32). He upholds His own in faith. Through His prayer they are preserved from the evil one. (John 17:15)

Just as Jesus prays for those in temptation, so also, on the basis of His consent, may the church pray for the preservation of her members and constantly admonish them to vigilance. Concern and prayer keep watch in every danger. The church dare not become sure of herself but must always keep the tempter in focus. Her vigilance consists in constantly praying against the tempter and in every situation considering what significance it has for the survival of the church. In prayer her eyes are opened to the dangers. In prayer she also receives courage and strength to face them (Luke 21:36). In prayer she also keeps herself aware that everything is at stake when a Christian is tempted. He has everything to lose and everything to gain.

Just as forgiveness has eschatological significance, so also does this testing. It is always eternal salvation that is involved (Mark 13:33 ff.). Only a nonpraying church can fall into self-confidence. But if the church is vigilant in prayer, she recognizes temptations before they appear. Nor may the church herself bring temptations about. She must not think she can stand in situations where other men fail. There is also such a thing as ecstatic faith, which leads to arrogance and thereby to a fall. Nor can the church sidestep existing temptations. She is privileged then to take up the battle trusting in the God who is on her side. He knows her strength, and He keeps her from falling. His faithfulness preserves her life (1 Cor. 10:13). Thus even in temptation the church experiences not only the power of the evil one but also the help and the reality of God. She knows that God Himself is fighting so that she may not lose salvation. He preserves the eternal inheritance for her. Thereby she receives such a great goal that she can be joyful in temptation. She is borne up by hope. (1 Peter 1:4-7)

Having redeemed mankind, God also rescues those who believe in Him. We could even say that *rescue in temptation is a part of His work of redemption;* for without God's preservation, without the presence of His Spirit, His people could not survive. The Lord of the Kingdom, who has made His own into citizens of the Kingdom, also preserves them for His coming kingdom. Temptations in themselves, therefore, are not tests and trials for the believers, but in the context of God's effective actions they are His preservation toward the eternal goal. How closely Christians are connected with God be-

111

comes evident when even in temptation they obey God and remain under His guidance.

If Christians do not prove themselves in temptations, they cannot proclaim the kingdom of God. When the faithfulness of God toward them does not work to make them faithful themselves, they dishonor God. If their disobedience becomes public, they obstruct the way for their fellowmen to believe in God. The church can serve the Lord only insofar as she herself lets Him act on her. If she falls into hypocrisy, her strength for missionary witness is lost. The church's ability to be salt and light decreases in the same degree that she falls into sin. Then she has nothing more to offer the world that it does not already have. If the church's concern for her own existence is more important than the mediating of redemption, then she is not capable of proclaiming the Gospel in a world hostile to God (Acts 20:19 f.). If she shrinks from temptation and suffering, Satan has already won his victory before he puts the church under pressure. Therefore the great times of peace for the church with their so-called great possibilities for mission work are above all a question to the churches themselves whether they understand their service rightly. When a church has made peace with the world, she is no longer led into temptation. Without knowing it she already lives in a kind of agreement with permanent temptation.

The servants of the church identify themselves by proving themselves in temptation and by carrying out the will of God in the midst of suffering (2 Cor. 11:23 ff.). When they follow God's guidance in this, He proves in the weakness of their lives His own immeasurable power. On the other hand, such a weakness can also become a temptation to a mission church that is brought up to live only on reports of success. The churches too want to see something impressive (Gal. 4:14). We live in an age when the difficulties in mission and church become a primary temptation to Christians. They cannot imagine that in extending His Word God could lead the church through temptation. If this happens, they believe that no more mission possibilities exist for them. They have so thoroughly adopted the principle that church and mission must represent the age they live in that they can no longer imagine a church under the cross. We no longer know anything of the blessing of poverty but think we must impress men by having even the church embody the material ideals of men. How superficially we equate the "love of Christ" with our progress in civilization and technology! The "love of Christ" is no longer measured by the words of Jesus but by the demands of men.

We have no idea how our example can be a temptation to the people of Asia and Africa. The connection between Christianity and Western civilization, as striven for by missions, has caused immeasurable damage. And yet we continue to think we must bring the people of Africa and Asia our Western form of Christianity. We take no thought that by personifying and realizing this example we make them socially more turbulent. We live among them as an image of something they can never attain because of their poverty. Should we then be surprised that for Africans and Asians Christianity remains something alien, which they describe as "the white man's religion"? When we pray, earnestly, "Lead us not into temptation," we should also pray that our human example and our standard of living might not be a temptation to others. In the time of the apostles the Gospel proved itself genuine and true in suffering. Today we want to win men by preparing the way for the Gospel with civilization and technology. We scarcely realize that thereby

113

we are playing the same role as the tempter played in the story of Jesus' temptation.

The church and consequently her missions here face significant questions. Is it right for her to swim along in the wake of the times instead of constantly asking herself how she should rightly administer and use her money? Can we really say that money belongs among the good gifts of God and that it is never misused in the hands of the church? We should of course be thankful that God upholds the work of His church and mission with the necessary money. With it He offers us possibilities that we can well use. Of this we need say no more. But we should ask ourselves what we must do *so that prosperity may not weaken the power of faith nor suppress our witness*. The latter happens only too easily when churches no longer have to be concerned for many things, nor are they thereby any longer led back to God. If this is the effect of money, then in spite of the church's great possibilities it has done more harm than good. Here too the church is not removed from temptation; on the contrary, precisely through her administration and practice she can herself become a temptation to her members.

In addition, there are a number of temptations appearing on the spiritual level that can bring a church's missionary prowess to defeat. Among these are, for example, the disputatiousness of pastors and the party spirit that destroys the unity of the church. Divisions weaken the church's strength and nullify the validity of her message before men. Divisions always arise in such a way that insights which God has granted to individuals are made absolute and charismata are misused as justification for one's own existence (1 Cor. 1:10 ff.). We generally base our church's work and missions on the thought that God has entrusted them with a special treasure that they

114

must maintain by their faithfulness to Him. According to the New Testament, however, insights and charismata can never serve as a person's own justification but only as preparation for service to the whole. Personal quarrels can have an even worse effect by destroying the spirit of brotherliness. When they appear, the Christian stance is forsaken. When repentance and forgiveness are no longer practiced, the basic elements of the life of Christian fellowship are destroyed. Thereby the doors are opened to Satan (2 Cor. 2:10-11). When such trends appear in a church, she can no longer witness effectively to the surrounding world. Such churches no longer attract but repel. We must learn that we can carry out mission only insofar as we take the Gospel seriously *within* the missionizing church.

In the case of this requirement two creeping temptations are gradually overcoming our churches. Since they live in a pluralistic society, church people are in great danger of gradually falling for other trends of the times, other world views and religions. *We live in an age when the uniqueness of the Gospel is no longer acknowledged.* In no other age has the brash premise that all religions are alike and that one can worship the same God in all of them been raised to such a level of dogma as today. Within our compass the other religions offer themselves to seeking men. Not a few expect from them the help that the church seems no longer to offer. The church no longer feels the authority to proclaim Jesus as the only One; thus He becomes one among many. In this way the other kingdom extends itself among us and seeks to displace the kingdom of God.

The other temptation appears in the church herself. The harder it is for her to approach men, the more she searches for new ways. Many of these ways lie outside

115

the Gospel or contrary to it. The Gospel is no longer the single, final authority for the church's practice. We determine the value of the Gospel according to what we can expect of modern man. Human reason has in a way made itself lord over Holy Scripture, for now we find ourselves asking whether there is any standard outside human existential understanding by which everything can be judged. Can the church, in such circumstances, still have a message valid for all if she does not return to the simple faith in Word and Sacrament and let God become Lord of her life? *Can a church still carry out mission if she has become uncertain in her message?*

When the church is so well adapted to the world, we can scarcely expect her to be able to pray the Sixth Petition with authority, both in view of her own service and in view of the young churches. How could it be possible to recognize the distresses of the young churches when we at home accept as perfectly natural the very things that are their temptations? How can our prayer be genuine if in their distress we do not recognize temptations that touch us also? The words about the hour of trial that is coming on the whole world is in this age of mass communications truer than ever (Rev. 3:10)! "Know that the same experience of suffering is required of your brotherhood throughout the world" (1 Peter 5:9). Thus likewise in this petition God includes us together with all men so that we may see how much we ourselves are in danger of succumbing to temptations. God has only *one* family. We cannot exclude ourselves from the petition, but are the first to be affected. If in this petition we were to forget our own temptation and look only on the young churches, as often happens in mission, we would then be hypocrites, judging others without recognizing our own distress. *Today every church lives in mission territory.*

116

The world of unbelief at home corresponds to the pagan surroundings in which the young church lives. The church of God is challenged by both. Previous history is at least as much a burden for the young church as is the Western spiritual history for the older part of Christendom. Therefore we can pray only in the unity of the church that God would preserve His people in temptation.

When intercession is genuine, the question of what help we can provide for others grows of itself. When Peter has given up his own volition and submitted himself to God, he receives the commission to strengthen the brethren (Luke 22:32). Strengthening, therefore, is possible only when we have received it from God and then pass it on. Paul saw this as his chief task next to proclaiming the Gospel. He used his missionary journeys to give assistance to those in tribulation, to mediate inner strength to them, and to direct them toward the time when their faith must stand the test in the fire of persecution (Acts 14:22; Rom. 1:11). Mission, therefore, does not come to an end with baptism and the founding of congregations. But neither does it continue as we have hitherto understood it, as if a congregation founded by a mission must always be directed by the mission. Service must shift over into brotherhood, in which the visitor shares with his brothers the gifts that he has himself received from his Lord. The mission's responsibility is now realized in its participation in the life of the young church. The mission shares her dangerous situation, suffers with her, and strengthens her inner life. The mission's assistance should make it easier for the young churches to make their own decisions, so that in the midst of temptation they can prove themselves to be the church of Jesus Christ. The mission's service remains even where the young church already exists. It is grounded in the faithfulness of God, who does not write off the congregation in tribulation nor give it up. God concerns Himself about it in such a way that He gives it over to the concern of other congregations.

In the midst of temptation missions see to it that faith stands the test. If God in His faithfulness confesses the churches in tribulation to be His own, then the missions have no right to give them up. How often it has come about since the end of the war that missionaries forsook their work and were returned home because difficulties and persecutions arose! They did not consider the fact that the Christians had to continue living under the same difficulties. We wish to make no judgment about such an attitude, but for the sake of the cause we must indicate that standing the test in the face of temptation has become very serious. Whoever allows God to pull him through tribulation is promised the gift of eternal life. (Matt. 24:13)

The missions have to stand the test of suffering because Jesus Himself suffers along with the church. Her suffering is always an explanation of His suffering. In her suffering He Himself suffers again and again for the world that has not yet accepted His redemption. Since Jesus Himself always stands the test of suffering, the suffering church may rejoice in His presence. Through Him God is always at the side of those who stand the test of temptation, and He guides them in such a way that the Gospel is extended through their suffering. The faithfulness and the confession of His church are rewarded by Jesus' own confession to them on the day of judgment. The suffering church clings to Jesus' promise that she is appointed to rule in kingly power (Luke 22:28 f.). There is no petition in the Our Father that does not have this eschatological reference. Every petition has to do with the final decisive element, the breaking forth of His kingdom and our participation in it in eternity. Only with this hope and this aim does the Sixth Petition attain its deep meaning.

Deliver Us from Evil

If temptation comes from the other kingdom, God's antagonist (Matt. 4:1), and becomes effective through the sinful nature of man, then the praying man's concern must be not to fall into the hands of the tempter and his fellow travelers. With God's help he must free himself from bondage to this other kingdom and place himself on God's side. The only possible way to do this is to pray; in prayer he confesses God as the Lord who is greater than the tempter. In the posture of prayer he also sees that everything contrary to the will of God is a temptation coming from the powers arrayed against God. Evil becomes for him the anti-God that threatens his own self. Thus in prayer he acknowledges evil itself and at the same time turns to Him who frees him from evil, overcomes it, or takes it into His service.

Above all *our petition confronts us with the incomprehensible reality of evil,* which men try to interpret offhandedly out of existence because it is uncomfortable for them to be connected with it in any way. Evil is a strange thing. The Holy Scriptures tell us as little about its origin as they do about the existence of God. It is simply there, just as God is there. The Christian's faith thus also includes the knowledge that there is a power inimical to God. "The questions that have to do with God and the demons have a degree of reality that far surpasses that of external historical factors, whether they be social, economic, or military. The invisible is mightier and also

119

more creative and destructive in history than the visible" (Thielicke, p. 118). The powers against God work against God's goal. They use God's creation in order to work against God. Thereby the church of Jesus desiring to do God's will becomes a battlefield. The battle rages of course in the rest of the world too insofar as it has not removed God from leadership. But the fight is not visible except in His church, where evil is part of the revelation that has come to her. Non-Christians can have an inkling of this battle, but they cannot explain it. Only the Holy Scriptures know that Satan and his works also stand under God's patience. Only the Scriptures know that in Jesus' final victory will Satan be defeated. The Scriptures know the kingdom where his works will be eliminated.

The Holy Scriptures do not think of evil abstractly. They do not speak in an abstract manner of God as if He could be proved and described in a philosophical fashion; nor do they speak of evil in itself, such as we see in theological works. Just as the Scriptures always speak of God only in His relation to men, so also evil is treated only in a way that somehow touches the man who is endangered by it. Just as man can experience God only through His revelation, through His speaking and acting in wrath, judgment, assistance, love, and redemption, so also he can recognize evil only in its effect on him. Evil too is a conscious will pursuing one aim with men, namely, to tear them away from God. That is why in the Holy Scriptures the devil is evil personified. In him it is all bound together and through him it becomes effective (John 8:44; 1 John 3:8). Therefore everything that turns against God must be understood as an expression of Satan. His gathering of forces is the reversal of the kingdom of God and can be understood and explained as the kingdom of Satan. (Matt. 12:22 ff.)

Satan also has his helpers. We never read in the Holy Scriptures that besides God there are other gods that can be taken seriously. But we do read that besides the devil there are other devils. Evil is thus separated into numerous anti-God powers that ultimately work together under one will. Just as God works through those who believe in Him and just as He makes the believers His co-workers, so also the devil has his dependents and servants. Most of them are not conscious of the fact that they are in his service. No one would confess the devil as his lord and thus admit that he was in the service of evil. When this happens in individual circles, we see the final perversion of religion. The especially tempting thing about Satan is that he acts in unity with human desires and wishes, so that his power appears to be a concern of men and a realization of the rights men lay claim to. He makes men themselves evil, but always by disguising himself with the claims of goodness. That is how he deludes men about himself. *Man can recognize this betrayal only when the Word of God has opened his eyes to it.* When we pray for deliverance from evil and thus pray against the evil one himself, we are then asking above all that God would open our eyes to recognize it. When we see it in its reality, we can pray very concretely that God would free us and protect us from it.

Satan is the great antipode of God, constantly interfering in God's work to obstruct God's lordship. The frightening thing for us is that God has not removed Satan's effectiveness from His church. The prince of this world will lead her into temptation so long as there is a church in the world. Wherever the Gospel is sowed as good seed, he also appears to sow weeds among the wheat. Where the Son of Man allows His servants to proclaim the message of salvation, Satan is also at work,

in all secrecy hindering the growth of faith (Matt. 13:
24 ff.). He mixes the sons of evil among the sons of the
kingdom of God so that the church can never present
herself before the world in purity as the church of the redeemed (13:37 f.). He misleads the believers, deceiving
them with the appearance of being good, of being marvelous, of being "willed by God." Since greatness impresses men, the church falls into this trap especially in
her choice of working methods. "What the tempter does
always has stature. It never lacks grand perspectives and
the touch of idealism" (Thielicke, p. 134). "Everything
the devil says is enormously positive. These are stupen-
dous goals, staggering in their persuasiveness" (ibid.,
p. 139). And it is all delusion, deception, intended to
keep Christians from their real task — their witness to
their Lord. Thus the devil destroys the church of God on
earth most often by showing her great possibilities and
giving her extraordinary means to fulfill them. He is no
dealer in rags.

The church's path, therefore, always skirts the edge
of apostasy. Her service is constantly endangered by her
desire to look rather to what the world offers than inquire after the will of God in her times. The devil wants
to lead her away from God with what he has to offer and
thus destroy her trust in God (John 17:15; 2 Tim. 4:18).
That is why Jesus calls His people to prayer and watch-
ing. He has come to destroy the works of the devil.
(1 John 3:8)

Thus prayer becomes a weapon in the battle against
the works and the temptations of the devil. *"The entire
substance of our prayer [is] . . . directed against our
arch-enemy"* (Large Catechism, Tappert, p. 435).
Through prayer the Christian can liberate himself from
his own sinful volition and from alien influences. He en-

trusts himself to God, and God commits Himself to him. By His presence God extricates His own from temptation and sustains them in their tribulation. He upholds them on the right path and grants them the strength to remain in His service and testify of Him as the only Lord. Whoever has once experienced the power of evil and God's liberating act from it should sin no more (John 5:14 ff.). If man were to remain under sin, he could no longer belong to the kingdom of God. Redemption would have happened in vain in his case. He would once more succumb to the body of death (Rom. 7:24; 8:22). When Jesus says that we should sin no more, it is possible only because by His death He has snatched us away from the kingdom of the devil (Eph. 2:2 ff.). We are granted a share in His victory. He will also bring it to pass that the devil is put under His feet.

This hope gives Christians strength. They know that the enemy is already conquered. In the strength of Jesus Christ they may therefore assist in destroying his kingdom. God lets them share in this battle through the service to which He has commissioned them. Seen in this perspective the proclamation of the Gospel becomes God's forced entry into Satan's dominion. The life of the church is the Lord's attack on the other realm of life in which God's commandments are not kept. The service of love is the means for combatting the destruction of God's creation. The praise of God among men robs Satan of his fame. In their joy and thanks to God the redeemed always remember those who are as yet unable to rejoice in God. God always leads His church so that through her He can make His mercy effective on the unredeemed world. Thus by the proclamation of the message of salvation He can snatch it away from the kingdom of darkness and incorporate it into His church. *Thereby God makes*

His mission an attack on the other kingdom and overcomes it through the faith and the witness of the church.
The proclamation of His Gospel among the nations is the
announcement of His victory. He sends His church to the
front. For the sake of the lofty goal He exposes her to
temptations, but He stays with her and gives her His
strength so that if necessary she can conquer even in defeat. Thus mission can be carried out only on the basis of
this profound bond with God.

Since the proclamation of the Gospel among the nations constitutes a prime attack on the devil's dominion
and on evil, it should come as no surprise to us that this
proclamation ignites evil's strongest defensive action and
its most powerful counterattack. The Christian must
therefore know the enemy he is challenging. He must
reckon realistically with this conflict, all the more so
since Jesus in His commissioning address did not leave
His followers in the dark about the subject. We must be
armed. In times of danger and persecution we may pray,
just as our Lord did, that the suffering might pass away.
On the other hand, however, we will learn as He did that
Satan is also provoked to action by prayer and that the
suffering can be intensified. But even then we are always
safe in God's hand.

Whereas the devil always works incognito to be able
to deceive men, God has founded His church by revealing Himself. He has made His name manifest. Now the
church can pray to God. She entrusts herself in battle to
God, and God commits Himself to her. Therefore in
prayer the church is able to exercise the watchfulness to
which her Lord has admonished her. She fights off evil.
In prayer she is able to stand up against the assaults of
the enemy and is thus privileged to experience God's
marvelous help. By God's action she is always a church

that perceives the power of evil in her witness, in service, and in suffering; by virtue of her suffering together with her brothers she draws the evil upon herself. Her struggle would be hopeless if God did not commit Himself to her. She travels her difficult path in the knowledge that she is carrying the Gospel among men in her Lord's place. Consequently, whatever she has to suffer is ultimately an assault against her Lord, and whatever she must do under tribulation, she always has her Lord as fellow sufferer. This parallel placement of Lord and church corresponds then also to the church's confession to her Lord's suffering and the victory of the One who is to come and bring full redemption for her.

This intimate fellowship finds its strongest expression in prayer. The church, standing in place of her Lord, is united with the will of her Lord and transfers everything to Him. That becomes apparent in a prayer such as in Acts 4:24 ff. The congregation prays with one mind to the Lord of heaven and earth, without whose will nothing happens (4:28). When the church yields to the will of her Lord, He through her prayer overcomes the mortal threat to her life. She prays as a church placing herself at His disposal, through whom He can work signs and wonders. She conceives of herself as an instrument. She knows that God can help even when from the human point of view everything is in vain. She has not yet used her reason to make God so small that she cannot expect the miraculous from Him. She is convinced that God always answers the prayer for the coming of His kingdom. A world opposed to God founders in the prayer of the church and in her Lord, through whom this prayer is heard and translated into action.

By the incessant prayer of the church the intrigues of Herod come to naught (Acts 12:5). Paul and Silas experience the effects of one such prayer. While they sing their hymn of praise to God, the doors of the prison are opened, the path for extending the Gospel is cleared. How often in the course of history have the doors to the nations been opened by prayer! The church has always had to prosecute its battle with the weapon of prayer, and the more she relied on prayer, the more she repelled the onslaughts of the devil. "Pray at all times in the Spirit, with all prayer and supplication. To that end keep alert with all perseverance, making supplication for all the saints and also for me, that utterance may be given me in opening my mouth boldly . . ." (Eph. 6:18 f.). A watchful church does not merely pray for herself and her members. She always remembers those who have been sent as her representatives among the pagans. She follows the course of the Gospel and accompanies it in prayer. A self-secure and prayer-impoverished church, however, succumbs. It is part of watchfulness that the church, by the extension of the Gospel, shares in what is happening in the world. She knows what is opposed to her. She keeps herself informed on what other congregations are doing. Thus by prayer and common suffering the church becomes a brotherhood under the Gospel. Her ecumenical reference finds expression in watchfulness, in common joy and common suffering, in common responsibility, and in intercession. Whoever knows the *oikumene* of faith and suffering stands also in the *oikumene* of prayer. In view of the entire church he is armed for the conflict with evil (1 Peter 5:8 f.). The church views herself as a link in a chain that encompasses the world — and that itself is already great encouragement for her. She never stands in solitude.

Thus the church becomes a fellowship of "comba-tants" (Zinzendorf). In prayer she breaks out of her repose and breaks through the fronts. She goes into the world of unbelief and proclaims with authority the message of her Lord even if she thereby encounters opposition and must suffer for it. The Our Father gives her the certainty that her Father, to whom she prays, also has power over evil. He can well put up with it; but that does not mean that He will let it endure. Time and again He rescues His church from evil. He conquers it with His might, and when it appears necessary to Him, He takes it into His service to punish the world with its own sins. He does not call forth evil, but wherever it arises it must eventually serve His purposes since He is the one and only Lord. This certainty is the foundation for the statement that in everything God works for good with those who love Him (Rom. 8:28). Thus God unites Himself with the praying church and directs everything in such a fashion that even under the efficacy of evil, in the church's suffering, His name is glorified.

Thereby suffering always means victory, as paradoxical as that may sound. The world will see how God subdues Satan for the church (Rom. 16:20). He Himself looks after the rights of those who have to suffer for the sake of His name. The world may well put the blame on the church outwardly and accuse her of having committed crimes. God, however, takes the part of those who call to Him day and night and vindicates them (Luke 18:7 f.). These are not merely eschatological assertions but promises that will be fulfilled in the life of the church. God is not an idle spectator when His church suffers and prays against her enemies. He takes her side in such a way that by the church's witness the accusers become the accused. This conflict will continue so long as there is a church of God on earth. According to the Revelation of St. John the conflict will not come to an end until Christ returns. So Christians can live in the confidence that the returning Lord will speak the last word in all things.

In this respect the last petition brings us back to the first three petitions of the Our Father. In praying for deliverance from evil we are praying for that which is God's. The final petition indicates the goal of God's action. With the destruction of evil God's kingdom will once again encompass everything that God has created. This ultimate goal should always shape the work of the church and her missions. How puny we often let mission work appear when we simply stand pat on the immediate goal of conversion! Mission in the view of the Holy Scriptures is only a means whereby God would achieve His ultimate goal. Our personal redemption is always a mere segment even though it is perhaps the center of the entire process of salvation introduced with the coming of Jesus and to be concluded with His coming again. God always has His eye on the entire creation. Into this fantastic expanse God has placed His church through mission. He makes mission into a cosmic event conditioned by the goal of history. But of course mission stands under the sign of God's patience (Rom. 3:25). This is decisive; for if there were no patience of God, there would be no mission. God's patience makes mission possible by postponing the judgment. In our prayer we always affirm God's love, which wants to rescue at the very moment when judgment ought to begin. Thereby our vision is directed exclusively toward God, who by His power subordinates also the evil to this goal.

6. For Thine Is the Kingdom . . .

The conclusion of the Our Father is not found in either of the original versions of the prayer. It was nevertheless appended quite early. It is normally understood as a hymn or doxology, just as we find similar doxologies in the apostolic epistles. Scholars say that in the Jewish prayer tradition it would have been impossible to end a prayer without such a conclusion. Thus the church also sensed the need to conclude the Our Father with a doxology. That may well have been one reason. Yet we should see more in the conclusion of the Our Father than simply a traditional hymn of praise. If Christian prayer is different from Jewish prayer, then one might expect that the conclusion of the Our Father also has a different meaning.

In some texts it is connected to the Lord's Prayer with the word "for." Therefore it is not merely understood as doxology but simultaneously as a grand statement of the foundations of this glorious prayer. By means of this the praying church — all Christendom — points to the evidence that justifies her praying to the Father. The assertions of the conclusion are the foundation and pre-supposition for her prayer and give her certainty for the prayer. If these assertions were not valid, the whole prayer would be empty phrases. The conclusion expresses the fact that everything belongs to God. All is at His dis-posal, and He has the power to intervene in history. As the Our Father relates the message of Jesus in brief, so the conclusion contains everything that the church has prayed, that she is privileged to request, and upon which her trust in God is grounded. He is in a position to bring honor to His divine name, and therefore He may also re-ceive from men their glorification of His name. His power is limited neither spatially nor qualitatively; it is bound to no time. He is able to exercise it at any moment without first asking someone's permission. He is not God just for a while. Neither is He dependent on the course of things. He is and remains the same from eternity to eter-nity. But He is not thereby a timeless God. Time exists only because He exists. He created it and gives it con-tent. He has seen fit to have the history of His revelation coincide with time. But time itself is only a small seg-ment of His unlimited being. And so amid all the changes of time He is the unchangeable One to whom His church, which lives in time, may turn. Even if she should pass away in her generations here on earth, He still remains the same in every generation and guarantees the continuity of His lordship and the extension of His Gospel in all generations. This will continue until the end of time and out to the limits of man's world. From the perspective of this God everything is conceived in univer-sal terms.

Thus the conclusion of the Our Father is our short-est doctrine of God. If it is invalid to base prayer on this, then every prayer is useless. But if it is valid, then the church with her prayer can conquer all through this God. If the assertions of the conclusion express the church's faith and conviction won in the encounter with God's revelation, then according to the Word of Jesus she is able to move mountains by her faith. It always remains questionable whether she will let Him bestow on her such faith and trust in His divine power and fatherly goodness. Our prayer is always conditioned by the degree of our trust in Him. "This word is nothing else than an unquestioning affirmation of faith on the part of one who does not pray as a matter of chance but knows that God does not lie since He has promised to grant his requests. Where such faith is wanting, there can be no true prayer" (Large Catechism, Tappert, p. 436). The more faith knows of the magnitude and love of God and is animated by it, the richer, more certain, more focused, and full of conviction will prayer also be. Some people find that their prayers provide them with the realization and confirmation of their faith. On the other hand, God is so great that He does not make the greatness of a man's faith the measure of His answer. He answers the poor prayer too — the stammering and the sighing. In fact He remains our God even when we can no longer pray. He grants His Spirit so that the Spirit can represent the petitioners. There are people who step by step have found God in prayer by letting Him draw them ever deeper into His mysteries.

Praising God is an assertion of the certainty of redemption. How far Christians really rejoice in their salvation can be seen in how and to what degree they praise God, thank Him, and wait patiently for His gifts. The believer prays to God and thanks Him for accepting him as His child and incorporating him into His kingdom in Jesus Christ. He is a child in the Father's household and a citizen of His kingdom. Thus in praising God he confesses his relationship to the Lord of the household and the Lord of the kingdom. In prayer God lets him experience the reality of the kingdom and rejoice in his status within it by virtue of the Word of promise. The Christian prays to the Almighty with whom nothing is impossible. He has the power. He does not belong to the "nobodies." However, the man of prayer also experiences God as the glorious One unmatched by any glory on earth and before whom he can only remain in adoration. He is permitted to perceive how this glorious One has condescended to him in His unending love. He has come so close to men that through Jesus Christ they can approach the very throne of His glory. In all of this, however, the believer finds a confirmation of his faith in the mighty acts of God whereby God achieved his redemption. So the Gospel makes the petitioner joyful, and he thanks God for speaking to him in Jesus Christ. In prayer he receives the certainty that God is a living, speaking, acting God. He remains in His actions the God who is always searching for man, revealing Himself, and standing by the witness and the service of the church.

God answers the petitioner in such a way that He assures him of His existence and His love. This testimony of God includes the certainty of prayer being answered, which for all those who come to faith through the proclamation is the surprise gift they previously did not have. It is based on the experienced nearness of God, who Himself makes the petitioner certain. If a man does not pray to God, he is unable to experience this presence. Ultimately he cannot even speak from inner conviction about the reality of God. As is the case in so much of the Christian life, so also here we must risk something in order to know the meaning (Matt. 7:7-8). In a certain sense this contradicts the current notion of faith that depicts it as an unconditional trust in God based exclusively on God's promise but not on human experience. But ultimately faith in this sense is the relationship to God that can still be justified before man's thinking reason. However, God addresses not only man's intellect but also his conscience and his emotions. If we ascribe no critical function to either of these, it is because neither one's critical function can be expressed logically. We tend to forget that the intellect with its critical and logical functions is at least as fallible as are conscience and emotions.

In any case God does not limit Himself to the humanly acknowledged path of knowledge. He makes His impact on man wherever the receptive organ is open to Him. He is not so radical as man; therefore He confirms Himself to man in prayer. In view of this the Holy Scriptures actually promote experience. We must ask in order to comprehend what receiving is. We are to seek to be able to find. We have to knock to pass through the door where God becomes reality to us. In all of this God is the exclusive Actor and Giver. Seeking always amounts to being found by Him. In this manner man is permitted to come to Him and from His fullness receive grace for grace. It depends therefore on us whether we will lay claim to the fatherly goodness or withdraw from God. In prayer God gives us a share in the riches of His house. He has everything ready for us that serves our salvation. He also bestows everything we need for our daily life as citizens in His kingdom. God also grants the resources for His work in His kingdom. His love to us is always the fulfillment of His mercy.

But God also is active with those who do not pray, who plod along worried by the cares of the day, anxious about their life, cowering before alien powers. They too stand under His care and live by His fatherly goodness. To His children, however, God has given peace of heart. He expects them to practice their rights as children and to ask Him as children ask their father. They receive and have what He has ready for them. They are permitted to receive when they ask. Thereby the carefree attitude expected of them takes on profound significance. It does not amount to indifference to the things of this world but is the highest responsibility. It is certainly not a sort of thoughtlessness that dissipates the gifts of God. By no means is it a fatalistic faith that surrenders gloomily and helplessly to the inevitable will of God without reacting to it in prayer. The carefree attitude required is the trust that God is directing things to His goal. Ultimately it means planning together with God, searching out His ways. Man can be carefree when he contemplates before God and together with Him what he as God's child must do to serve the divine goal. Being carefree amounts to taking God seriously in all decisions. In prayer we fit ourselves into God's will and thereby participate in the highest that God wants to give us — His love.

Implicit in this is the statement that an answer to prayer cannot mean the fulfillment of our wishes but rather the willingness to acknowledge God's actions toward us and with us. God's will must happen to us before it can be fulfilled through us. *Thus everything God enjoins becomes a commission intended to become witness.* For example, God can leave a man in serious sickness and nevertheless answer his prayer since he becomes so willing and strong to radiate in his weakness the strength and glory of God that the people around him perceive it (2 Cor. 12:7 ff.). God can allow misfortune in order to reveal Himself in the act of rescue as the Lord of life and of nature (Rev. 27:22). Although we may be of the opinion that God appears silent in the momentously fateful blows that often determine history, nevertheless He is still patiently at work. God also leads things in such a fashion that He does not fulfill our wishes, especially when we think we can claim something special by virtue of our profession or our position. Instead of turning our back on His guidance we must realize in the very moments when He does not support our self-chosen ways that His ways are still open to us. He always directs us beyond our own selves and is not content to have His grand goals perverted by our personal wishes. Just as with Him everything originates in eternal love and culminates in eternal glory, so our lives should also point toward eternity. For this reason praising God and thanking Him always means viewing things and the course of events from the vantage point of the goal and letting God's eternal love surround us.

The doxology of the Our Father also includes the church's gratitude. As she derives every justification for prayer from God and from His fatherhood, so she ascribes to Him in thanks everything He has done for her. Thanks in this case is not only expression of dependence, of piety, or of a specific inner attitude but acknowledging God's activity in our lives and in history. Thanksgiving prevents us from taking everything thoughtlessly and as a matter of course. The person who is thankful gives God the glory. Therefore every answered prayer should have a response of thanksgiving (Luke 17:11 ff.). The ungrateful person constantly puts himself in the center and does not want to accept responsibility for what he has received by expressing his thanks for it. It is in thanksgiving that God is glorified and praised because it always amounts to a proclamation of the acts of God, as is richly demonstrated in the psalms of praise and thanksgiving. For this reason thanksgiving is in first place in the prayers of St. Paul. He never ceases to thank and praise (1 Thess. 1:3; Eph. 1:16). *Whoever does not cease to thank is also constant in prayer.* From thanksgiving comes also the courage to approach God anew. On the other hand, the man who has forgotten how to give thanks runs the danger of growing dull in prayer or else never getting beyond superficial requests. When man refuses to give God praise, God is no longer a reality for him. For Paul thanksgiving for what God has done among men through the Gospel is at the head of the list. Thereby the glorification of God also takes on a missionary motive.

The pagans do not know the Gospel; therefore the glorification of God that occurs in thanksgiving is alien to them (Rom. 1:21). They stand under God's activity, and yet they trace nothing back to Him, ascribing it instead to other powers. Thus their thoughts remain imprisoned in nothingness. They know of thankfulness, but they do not give glory to Him who alone deserves it. Thus one might use thanksgiving to describe the proper relationship to God. Thanksgiving is the response of man to what he has received from God, a response to the relationship that God has brought into existence. Thankless men are basically lost men since they have not accepted the love of God. Mission rescues men from this condition. Paul therefore describes the content of the mission to the heathen as the cause of their glorifying God. (Rom. 15:9)

The conclusion of the Our Father also sets us in the vast fellowship of those who pray. Although the word "us" is missing, doxology always involves the whole church. *We cannot glorify God if we are unwilling to belong to His people on earth.* Confessing faith in God is always a confession of the congregation of believers, which God has brought into existence through redemption. As important as personal Christianity is, it is a distorted abbreviation when confined to the concepts "God" and "the soul." When God accepts us, he relates us also to the others who believe in Him and have been put into service by Him. The glorification of God always directs us beyond ourselves to those who have received the same things as we have. The New Testament does not speak in the language of the solitary individual, but in the plural. That is why the great liturgies of the church speak in the "we" form, which alone is capable of expressing the praise of God.

The glorification of God cannot achieve its full validity if the "we" form is understood in an exclusive sense. *The "we" places us once more into solidarity with all mankind, for whom God's church praises Him vicariously and in joyful anticipation.* Behind genuine doxology stands the desire to have all men participate in it. Thus doxology once more points us directly to the missionary task. The doxological church keeps in mind the men who are unable to praise God. So long as they are not involved our doxology remains incomplete. In regard to them the church has a privilege that obligates her since God would have this doxology from His entire creation.

No one can glorify the name of God and thank Him for everything he has if he is not ready in the "Amen" to express his own certainty of his prayer being answered. The Amen is assurance not only that everything is in God's hands but also that He has accepted the prayer. With his Amen the praying man indicates that he wants to be included in the action that his prayer instigates.

137

*God answers prayer in such a way that He always in-
cludes the petitioner in what he has asked from Him.* If
the petitioner expects God to answer his prayer — which
is the only way his praying makes sense — then he cannot
act contrary to that which he has requested. In his prayer
he has given everything over to God and yet made it his
own affair so that he can no longer retreat from it. So the
petitioner himself participates in the answer to his prayer
and can rejoice in the fulfillment of the promise.

What has been said applies also to the doxology of
the church. Every doxology would amount to empty
words if the church refused to let God renew her. If she
acts against God's will and limits His jurisdiction, then
He to whom she has ascribed the kingdom, power, and
glory cannot be the one who is really in her midst. God is
not present alongside the church but in her. Thus the
church can only praise God by remaining in His realm of
activity. In this fashion the conclusion of the Our Father
refers us back to the first three petitions. What was
prayed for there as God's own action must find space
within the church herself.

The entire life of the church has the ultimate goal
of proclaiming God as the Lord of all men and offering
them redemption in Jesus Christ. God approaches men
by being proclaimed to them. Thus He becomes their
God. They are brought home to the Father. This does not
mean that all men receive the message and follow the
call into the kingdom of the Father. Mission can never be
anything but an offer. To make the offer is the task of the
church. It will take Christ's return to achieve the visible
redemption and completion. Then the power of evil will
be banished. Everything will belong to Christ, who will
rule at the direction of His Father (Rev. 12:10). Into His
kingdom will be taken those who believed in Him on

earth. They will shine like the sun in the kingdom of the Father (Matt. 13:43). They will participate in the royal rule (Luke 22:29). Then they themselves will be surrounded by some of the glory that they have seen with the Father.

These glorious promises indicate God's goal with men. To be able to make this gift to men, God carries out the commission in His Son and through Him sends forth the emissaries of the kingdom. He unites us to this sending and thereby grants us the highest commission He can give to men. The missionary command remains the most magnificent commission ever granted. When it is accepted, the mission always points toward the consummation that God has ready. His church will live in His glory because He will be all in all.

7. The Prayer for Mission

If we comb the New Testament for assistance in missionary prayers, we notice initially that we have no report about special mission prayers in the churches. Without question they existed. We know that the congregation in Antioch prayed for its missionaries. We also know that Paul admonished the churches to pray for special aspects of the extension of the Gospel. However, apart from the passages in Acts 4:23-31 and 12:5 and 12 we have no further presentation of mission prayer. We are surely not in error if we assume that the prayer of the early church always had a missionary dimension. The churches of the New Testament had to understand themselves as *combatant congregations*. They could not live out their faith in their pagan environment without trouble. They certainly could not expect to go unnoticed by other men. In contrast to contemporary Western Christianity the congregations of that time, like the young churches today, had to witness to their faith. Attacks arose from their environment which brought temptation, led to oppression, and was intent on preventing the Christian faith from getting a foothold. The churches led such an insecure existence that their future lay only in the missionizing of their environment. They became dynamic centers impelled to challenge their environment with a life conditioned by Christ. Since the congregations of Christians believed, lived and testified to the assertion that Jesus Christ is the only Lord and Redeemer, their very existence amounted to the sharpest criticism of pagan religion. We can hardly describe how harsh a criticism the pagans find the Gospel to be when it is lived by a congregation. The churches were forced into conflict with their environment because the adherents of the other religions somehow had to come to terms with the congregations of Christians. In this reciprocal struggle many violent clashes occurred. Therefore we can hardly conceive of the prayer of these churches as having no missionary dimension. There was no special mission prayer because the churches' prayer life per se was conditioned by mission.

When something special occurred, it was communicated by the apostles to the congregations. The congregations were called upon to pray for the messengers of the Gospel or to meet the new situation in prayer. Since in the New Testament we have no reports from the congregations — only the writings of the apostles and evangelists to them — it is understandable that little is reported about the prayer life of the congregations. The actual wealth of references to prayer is therefore with the apostles. From their prayer life we learn how they cared for the course of the Gospel and the life of the congregations. Above all they convey how their stance toward the churches was determined by their prayers. The latter is especially important for us since we too stand as mission vis-à-vis the young churches. The apostles found the proper relation to their churches in prayer. On the basis of the manifold references to this we could compose a doctrine of missions and develop the relationship between missionary and congregation, between missionizing Christianity and young churches.

We find ourselves in an age when the missions live in a certain tension with the young churches. It has arisen as the young churches have removed themselves from under the leadership of the missions. Depending on the circumstances in the various territories, they take the position that they as the church in that particular place have to carry the responsibility for missionizing their surroundings. As a result the missionary from the older Christianity can carry on his work only within the young church and in cooperation with her. Many Western missionaries have not yet reconciled themselves to this situation. It is characteristic that till now the missions have hardly begun any theological clarification of the relationship between mission and young church, which ought to have been expected much sooner since they represent the very circles that hold God's Word in high esteem. Till now, however, they have not applied the assertions of the New Testament to their concrete situation. Thus since 1920, when this development began, missions have been caught in an experiment that is slowly depriving them of their authority for action.

The missions from the West, America included, were so strongly conditioned by the feeling of white racial superiority that the thought never occurred to them that the path from top to bottom, which always began with the superior position of the missionary, could possibly be wrong. They often coupled the proclamation of the Gospel with the expansion of the Western form of Christianity. Frequently social progress replaced the inner life so that when judged by such social standards the young churches always had to take a back seat. Today the young churches object to these tendencies. They want to achieve a relationship with the missions that finds its expression in Christian brotherhood and equal rights. Much unconfessed and unforgiven guilt remains between the parties, so that we must ask how a genuine integration of church and mission is possible on the basis of such tensions. Integration will not come until both partners recur to the New Testament and draw their directives from it.

If we have understood the Gospel correctly, everything it offers us and what our work can derive from it is *described as God's work*. This basic insight conditions the relationship of the apostles to their churches. In the foreground therefore is not the question of authority, even though it is an extremely burning issue in Corinth and Galatia, but the apostles' commission from God and consequently their gratitude for being allowed to stand in the service of the Gospel. For Paul everything else appears secondary. He is overwhelmed by the glorious gift of the Gospel entrusted to him by God for the rescue of mankind. Therefore he does not defend an institution, not even that of his office, but only this gift. He is all wrapped up in what the Gospel accomplishes among men. Daily he turns himself over anew to God's power contained in the Gospel and to God's love working its wonders in the lives of Christians. Paul does not therefore begin with the legal question in viewing his relation to the congregations. He does not consider mission his monopoly. He is only a deputized agent. As such he is re-

144

sponsible to Him who called him into His service. God is the one who carries out His sending.

D. T. Niles once said that we men do not bring God and His Gospel to men but that He brings us as the gift of His love so we might proclaim Him. Thus mission gets God's grand priority. He uses the apostle as His instrument and equips the instrument for His service. So Paul can pass on to men the knowledge that he himself has been granted. God therefore remains the sender and the executor. Only because He is at the apostle's side can Paul participate in the victory of Jesus Christ despite his physical weaknesses and his suffering. For Paul mission is Christ's grand triumphal procession in which he himself marches along as prisoner (2 Cor. 2:14). He himself is the conquered one who now stands in the service of Jesus. As such he contributes by his service to the glorification of Jesus. But he is not the lord of mission who can manage the fruits of his own work and relish his reputation. He is but one of many whom Jesus in similar fashion has conquered and won for His work. Where mission is so understood, self-ambition is eliminated. All is absorbed in the will of God.

In this perspective *mission becomes a gift of God to His church*, received together with the gift of the Gospel. Through the Gospel the entire church comes under God's preferential priority. As a matter of fact the Gospel has actually come to her through the emissaries of Jesus Christ and not yet to other men. It has been entrusted to her as the message intended for all men. If she does not pass it along, she incurs a debt with the men to whom the Gospel also belongs. The assignment to pass it along is not only a command but even more an authorization. The church is put into service ever anew by her Lord. She is called. That amounts to being favored by God. For this reason thanksgiving is predominant in Paul because God has selected him for His service. He has been taken into the mercy of God, and this mercy now animates him. By their calling God's messengers become mediators of mercy. Their office is based on their own encounter with mercy (2 Cor. 4:1). They themselves were lost men. Like others they lived in darkness. They too did not know the way of God. But now God has had mercy on them. By their calling all this now lies in the past, and yet it conditions their service in decisive measure.

Since they have experienced what rescue through Jesus Christ is, they also know that they dare not retain the message of Jesus for themselves. They are animated by the conviction that Jesus died for all and that He wants to rescue all. On the basis of this fact they do not offer men an empty, diffuse word, but they stand before men as examples of the mercy of God which they are commending. They do not forget their past; for if they give it no thought at all, they would be unable to comprehend what has happened to them in their calling (1 Tim. 1:12-17). They may now however work in the certainty that the Lord who has conquered their own stubborn hearts and liberated them from their sinful lives can also renew and redeem those to whom they bring the Gospel. Thus they have a share in the victory of Jesus Christ and are themselves examples of the saving grace of the Gospel. Although they were unworthy, yet Jesus has made them strong, acknowledged them as trustworthy, and placed them into office (1 Tim. 1:12). For Paul this is the great mystery that keeps triggering his thanksgiving. They work not only under assignment of Jesus Christ but also in His power. The more they dedicate themselves to it, the stronger this power becomes in them and the more effective it becomes on the men to whom they proclaim the Gospel. The grace of God becomes visible (1 Cor. 15:9-11). Paul cannot give thanks enough for it.

This fundamental experience conditions the relationship of the apostle Paul to his congregations. The Gospel has demonstrated the same power with them. They have come to faith just as the apostles did. Thus the same miracle has occurred. They received the Word of God, and now it is unfolding its power in them (1 Thess. 2:13). Because of the Word's effectiveness the apostles have no preferred position. The congregations stand together with them on the same level; both find themselves under the efficacy of the same Word. Both are demonstrations of God's one mercy and His saving action among men. Since the effects of the Gospel in this manner become visible on both sides, the apostle has no cause for despair in his missionary service. *Whoever has experienced the power of the Gospel in his own life knows how it works in all men.* Whoever knows its power is not depressed because of weaknesses in the congregations. The Gospel always provides joy for further service. Since God's Word does bear such fruit, the apostles also have no cause for being ashamed of proclaiming it. It shows itself everywhere to be the power of God for salvation to everyone who believes it (Rom. 1:16). The position of Jesus Christ's messengers may be attended by tribulation and opposed by men. That makes no difference. What is important is the fact that God's power is their legitimation.

In mission everything appears as God's act. Conversion, faith, and new life are produced by God alone. He alone therefore merits the praise and thanks. In contrast to self-glory Paul always points to what God does. But God works among men the same way He worked on the apostles. Peter too confirms this: "By His great mercy *we*

147

have been born anew to a living hope" (1 Peter 1:3). Here too the newly won are included with the apostle. The latter has nothing that the congregations do not also have. They all stand under the same effective action and under assignment of the one Word since all have received the same gift from God. Solidarity under the Word and in the reception of salvation incorporates all believers into one unity. *From this common, fundamental experience the apostles' relationship to the congregations is determined.*

It should be the same way with the relationship between mission leadership and the young church, missionary and congregation, the missionizing church at home and the Christians abroad. There are no opposites, no superior and inferior, no givers and receivers. Both are a unity before God even if they have different tasks and obligations. No one can pride himself on his own deeds. All that anyone can do is worship, marvel, and give thanks in the face of what God has initiated and carried out through His Word. How many tensions between the mission and the young churches would have been eliminated if this common basis had been the point of departure! How much greater the mission's authority could be in the face of tribulation if this were the basis on which decisions were made! He who has experienced that God does everything is able to place everything in God's hands, day after day, with the certainty that His power will indeed show itself anew in time of need. Missionaries with this conviction are never helpless. The more they have learned to thank and pray, the more established they are in their position.

Thus we can say that the apostles' relationship to their congregations is shaped by their fellowship in the Gospel, by receiving grace, and by being called. This gives them their authority, which we need discuss no further since it is already disproportionately emphasized by the concept of office dominant today. But woe to us if we let this concentration on the pastoral office kill our awe before the works of God, which manifest themselves in power and in the Holy Spirit and in the full conviction attending the proclamation! (1 Thess. 1:5). The miracle of God's love is so great in the eyes of the apostles that they themselves are supported by it. The more they are able to make this visible, the more authority they have. The preacher who lets God alone do the speaking and acting always has the greatest authority. This does not render the messengers of the Gospel helpless vis-à-vis men but bestows on them a primary position. If they have God's Word backing them up, they do not need the support of human authority, which is usually nothing more than an expression of man's will for self-assertion. The Gospel unites both. It binds the apostles to the congregations and the congregations to the apostles. Here too we see the relationship within the framework of a divine household.

It is significant that the apostle Paul compares his position with that of a father. This of course has absolutely no connection with the paternalism that has become common in missions. The reality of a gift of grace cannot be bent into the shape of a manageable institution. *The father concept pinpoints the essence of the matter.* As God in Jesus Christ has become Father to all those who believe in Him, so Paul has become father to those to whom he has preached the Gospel and who through him have come to faith. To lead someone to faith means to beget new life, to initiate in the Holy Spirit the process of new birth. By virtue of the newly given life from God the messengers of the Gospel become

149

fathers. The fatherly relationship to the churches is thus not without pain and concern. It is not expected that the children practice a docile obedience. The concerns arise not in the realm of reciprocal relations but in the things that happen to hinder or destroy the new life. To maintain new life, to help it come to maturity, to awaken it anew and unfold it where necessary is very much like the process of birth, in which the father has many anxious moments of inner distress about the life of the children (Gal. 4:19). With new life the issue is not the private wishes of the missionary. What is important is that Christ be formed in men. Thus Christ is the measure of all things, not some pattern of religious life that may be close to the heart of the missionary. The form of Jesus Christ is the only standard for judging younger Christians, not what we in Christendom have made out of the Gospel.

Since God alone bestows the new life, the fatherly role of the missionary is always one derived from Him. This gives the missionary his own worth. By virtue of his position toward the congregation he does not do the same thing that other men do. He does not assume the role of civil servant or educator. Although the entire recent period of mission history and the relationship of missionaries to young Christians has been conditioned by the pedagogical perspective, Paul views his preferred position as the privilege of being a father and not the necessity of being an educator. He does not deny that there can be educators under Christ. But he knows that his relationship to the congregations dare not be determined by pedagogical perspectives. The teacher always stands above or apart from those whom he is teaching. He does not necessarily have an inner relationship to them. His task requires him to view those whom he is teaching differently from the way he views himself. For his task he carries a certain blueprint in his heart, which he does not necessarily have to incorporate in himself. The relationship between teacher and student is an artificial one. The relationship of father to children is one determined by life itself. Vis-à-vis the children Paul would like to be a father in Christ (1 Cor. 4:15). The father's eyes view the children differently from the teacher's. The children cannot be envisioned without some connection to the father. He too sees the errors of the children and suffers under them. He does not come upon the errors by comparison with some specific pedagogical ideal, but he measures the children by the sonship they have been given in Jesus Christ.

The father looks first of all at the developing life, at the growth. He rejoices over that which God lets develop. The father is bound to the children in love, and he addresses them on the basis of paternal authority. He makes obedience easy for the children since he knows they will acknowledge him as a genuine father only if he lives out before their eyes what he requires from them. He leads them to Christ in such a way that he bids them become imitators of himself (1 Cor. 4:16; 1 Thess. 1:6). Thus he is certain that his very person portrays discipleship of Jesus Christ. He lives out discipleship before the eyes of his Christians in such a way that they can reproduce it in their own situations. He does not live an alien life that the Christians in their own culture could never appropriate as a model. He makes it easier for them to be obedient. Consequently no schism arises between what the father does and what he expects of his children. For both parties the Gospel remains the unifying element.

On the basis of this position Paul leaves his congregations in neither external nor internal dependence. He

151

always focuses attention on what God has achieved in himself and in the congregation. Thus, for example, he can acknowledge among the Corinthians the enrichment of life (1 Cor. 1:5) that is present even at the very spot where it is in danger of being smothered by the filth of sin. He does not succumb to the precipitate conclusion that wherever instances of sin occur, as in the Corinthian congregation, life from God can no longer be present. He knows too that he can add nothing to that life as God has bestowed it. Whatever is lacking in such life God Himself must always supply. He is the only one who can bring to completion what was once begun (Phil. 1:6). Thus Paul allows his congregations the right to pass through their own specific laws of growth. Each Christian generation has its own gift and its own assignment from God. How unfairly we often treat the young churches by measuring them according to what we understand by Christianity! We forget in the process that we are dragging along with us the entire "volume" of Western church and dogmatic history, and on the basis of it we often rely more on our historical heritage than on the actual facts of faith and life in our churches. Dare we measure the young churches by such yardsticks? They necessarily appear unfair to the degree that they leave the decisive question unanswered, namely, what it would look like to be a disciple of Jesus Christ in the context of a different culture. Here too the only valid answer is that the form of Jesus alone can be allowed to supply the guidelines.

Paul is not blind to the weaknesses of his congregations. But he does not put them under the spotlight of his theology. Instead he places the congregations before the face of God, the only source from which new life can come. He views them under the love of God that is operative everywhere. Through his prayers he therefore carries the congregations in his heart. *In intercession he finds the right measure.* Since God is no respecter of persons, He is unable to view any of His Christians as minor or lower-class members of the body of Christ. They are permitted to stand before God in their own stage of growth and to wear the shape that God Himself lets develop in the process of growth itself. They are always fellow participants in the grace the apostle himself has received (Phil. 1:7-8). This conditions the relationship. Paul does not apply laws of biological growth to his congregations. Aging has significance on the basis of the New Testament only when it is understood in the sense of maturity. In maturing, however, fruit is produced. This is not tied to biological automatism but solely to faith and obedience. In the center of the apostle's perspective stands the new life, which as God understands it is always perfect life. That is the apostle's concern. That is what he wrestles about in prayer.

Inwardly he is also with those whom he does not know. He is struggling for them just as much as for those who are personally bound to him. He extends his pastoral care to all. His trip to Rome, for instance, is not an inspection tour, but he comes to the Roman Christians as one richly blessed and wanting to share something of his spiritual gifts with them. He is traveling in the expectation that he himself might receive something in mutual exchange (Rom. 1:10-20). He is not making the trip in some sense of superiority as though only he had something to bestow. He knows that God can enrich him through whatever He has allowed to develop in the congregations. Thus a brotherhood relationship arises. Therein Paul acknowledges what happens via the young church. She has followed the example of the apostles and

of the Lord, having received the Word in tribulation and
with joy in the Holy Spirit, and has become such a model
for all believers that her radiant missionary power extends everywhere. Thus the young church by the mere
fact of her existence is a missionary factor (1
Thess. 1:6-8). These are not empty words of praise. Here
the young church is acknowledged in the efficacious action of the Gospel. She is permitted to be what God has
determined she shall be. For this she does not have to
have any certificate of maturity from the older missionizing church. Paul views everything from the common
basis of God's efficacy and thus in the light of a life process where superiority and subordination do not exist.
Thereby the posture of Christian obedience is not ex-
cluded. It was the Thessalonians who had to prove themselves in suffering. Yet where the proper attitude is present, obedience becomes no burden, but joy arises
through the Holy Spirit.

Since Paul's line of vision is first of all directed to
the effects of the Gospel in the congregations standing
amid a pagan environment, he does not indulge in any
black-white painting in his epistles. Even where the situation in the congregation is blameworthy and where
congregations cause him considerable internal distress
and anguish he can still speak of the saints and thank
God for them and for the life granted to them. *For Paul,
honoring God includes recognition of what he himself
still does in a sinful congregation.* Even where his authority is questioned and the congregation is splitting into
splinter groups he can speak of the riches of life (1
Cor. 1:1-9). The posture of thankfulness preserves him
from bitterness, since from it he can view the affairs in
Corinth apart from their implications for his own person.
Thus the Corinthians receive a wide space in his heart

(2 Cor. 6:11 f.). He rejoices that they are strong (13:9). The reports he receives about the congregation not only give him pain but impel him to thanksgiving and intercession. He also thanks God that the news of the faith of the Roman congregation has gone into all the world (Rom. 1:8). His joy over the congregational life in Ephesus and over the faith and love of the Ephesian Christians expresses itself in thanks to God (Eph. 1:15-17). He cannot think of the Philippian congregation without giving thanks (Phil. 1:3 f.). The same is true about the Colossians and Thessalonians (Col. 1:3 f.; 1 Thess. 1:2; 2 Thess. 1:3; 2:13). Such an inner attitude is possible only if the Gospel messenger has his eye glued not to his small work area but to all the churches; in other words, if he is permeated by the universal claim of the Gospel. Paul rejoices that the Gospel is bearing fruit everywhere and bringing men redemption. He follows its course through the world, and its effects gladden his heart. These reports strengthen his own faith; the truth of the Gospel is confirmed for him. All this removes Paul's work from the small broken-check pattern of egocentricity and makes it part of the grand movement that originates in God.

Prayer is a concomitant of thanksgiving. *When men have occasion to give thanks, they receive the joyfulness to pray.* Intercession opens Paul's eyes to the conditions in the congregations. He discovers so much of the great and good in them that what he has to admonish does not get specially mentioned in the prayers. Nevertheless it was included in his intercessions. It moves him to such an extent that it finds shape in the closing sections of his letters. In prayer, however, the gifts come to the fore. God has equipped the congregation with all speech, all knowledge, and all spiritual gifts (1 Cor. 1:5-7). They have faith and love for all the saints (Eph. 1:15). They

155

are partners in proclaiming salvation (Phil. 1:5). Among the Colossians the Gospel is bearing fruit; they have understood the grace of God in truth (Col. 1:6). Their life is hid in God (3:3). Thus for Paul these congregations are not immature. He does not tell them: "You are not yet far enough along. You cannot do that yet. You are much too poor for that." To him they are all coequal Christians in the body of Christ. He is not looking for copies of his own faith. He guards against having his work become a standard method or routine schedule. Therefore he does not seek to lord it over the Christians and lead them on a leash. He rejoices much more at being their co-worker, while more recent missions have at best viewed the new Christians as their assistants. In similar fashion Peter sees himself as a "fellow elder" (1 Peter 5:1). In short, the apostles work with the congregations and fit themselves into the totality.

In terms of the New Testament, however, acknowledging the autonomy of the congregations and respecting their life and decisions certainly does not mean that they can do all things apart from the rest of the fellowship. By this very acknowledgment they are always simultaneously placed within bounds and into continuity with the church. One can see this in the New Testament in the way everything spoken to individual congregations can always be appropriated by the entire church. Correspondingly, when the entire church is addressed, it has meaning for every congregation. Just as it contradicts God's leadership and the guidance of the Holy Spirit to keep congregations on a leash and to make our own convictions the standard for all, so on the other hand it is incompatible with divine sonship for Christians to ignore the admonition of their brothers. Therefore Paul opposes the presumption and the inflated egos of the Christians in

Corinth, just as he compels them to make their own decisions in all things. The two do not contradict each other. Decisions must always be bound to God. Presumption and pride, however, eliminate God. Their chief concern is man's glory and not God's ways. Whoever rejects brotherly admonition refuses to subordinate himself to the will of God.

Paul wages his battle against false teachers and sinners not for the sake of his apostolic authority but as one responsible for the congregations. He helps straighten out the theological issues and makes the congregational conscience responsible for decisions about correct doctrine. In addition he admonishes them to submit to the leadership of the elders. Thus they should obey the authorities whom they themselves have elected (1 Cor. 16:18; 1 Thess. 5:12; 1 Tim. 5:17). It is Paul's concern to support the authority of those who have been called to lead the congregation. He only desires to be their assistant. His constant goal is to make the congregations strong so that their life can exemplify to non-Christians what the Gospel has achieved among them.

This by no means implies that Paul was unaware of the elders' sins and the failures of the congregations and had never opposed them. He could speak up passionately for purity of life. He was in close contact and well informed. Even in prison he remained the missionary concerned about his congregations. He maintained contact from prison and very likely struggled more for the salvation of his congregations in this situation than many a clergyman who serves in freedom! Paul also knew that faith, love, hope, and the Christian life with its many spiritual gifts are no secured possessions. He himself encountered time and again the power of evil in his own body and in his work. No tribulation was alien to him.

He was acquainted with the power of paganism, the demonic powers, and the ideologies that influenced the congregations. But he was at the same time convinced that God with His Spirit stands by His church in every situation and leads her to stand the test if she remains open to His Spirit.

Genuine intercession is effective only if the praying man knows the needs of the people for whom he wishes to pray. He must also be prepared to acknowledge God's actions and support His ways. For example, genuine intercession is impossible if one clings to an antiquated picture of missions and longs for something of the past that no longer has any place in God's guidance. *Intercession means standing entirely in the existing state of affairs and reflecting on the paths God now wishes to take with His church.* Where congregational life is measured by an imaginary picture of what missions ought to be, no accurate judgment can possibly be made. Then it is all too easy to overlook the forces with which God is working in the present. The many black-white portraits in mission reports are the products of a false perspective. It often comes to pass that the Christians learn more of what the devil does than what God's Spirit is achieving among them. That certainly does not serve to honor God. Neither can these presuppositions result in genuine pastoral care because we then overlook the help God has already given. The prayer life of the apostle Paul always reveals the heart of the missionary. His prayer is imbued with love and mercy. It is noteworthy that in the apostle's intercessions his prayer for protection from sin does not stand in the foreground. Nevertheless it is there since he asks for the very gifts which, if granted, would bring about protection from sin. He prays, for example, for the strengthening of congregational life (1 Cor. 1:8) and for congregational faithfulness (1 Thess. 3:13). He also prays that the congregations be delivered from the wicked men who are destroying them (2 Thess. 3:2). Paul also knows, however, that the failure of the Christians is more often the result of an internal attitude than the consequence of some outside interference. Even the Christian structures his actions according to the wishes of his heart. For this reason it is most necessary that he receive inner direction through the Word of God. The renewal of his mind and the sharpening of his conscience are what count. That is what Paul strives for. Thus his intercessions fall into four categories: right knowledge, right faith, eternal inheritance, and glorification of God.

The proper practice of the love of Christ depends on right knowledge. It consists not only in specific intellectual perception and the corresponding insight but combines with both the inner wisdom that determines a man's attitude. *Knowledge is intellectual perception that has been thought through in faith and purified by prayer.* Man can receive this as a gift only through the Word of God. Through this gift conscience receives a norm and the understanding a criterion. If a man is equipped to test what is right, he can also know the will of God. The fruits of righteousness grow from the illumination of God's Word (Phil. 1:9-11). It is not always easy to know the will of God clearly, and yet in companionship with God's Word man can arrive at the point where he is certain of his way. This too is a matter of prayer. Paul therefore prays that the Colossians be filled with the knowledge of God's will in all sprirtual wisdom and discernment (Col. 1:9). The right knowledge of God's will depends on the right knowledge of God and on the right conduct of the Christians. Only the Christian who strives to understand God in everything will also be equipped with the power to bring forth fruits of faith and lead a life worthy of the Lord (Col. 1:10 ff.). The apostle Paul's co-worker Epaphras prays earnestly for the Colossians that they "may stand mature and fully assured in all the will of God" (Col. 4:12). The issue, therefore, is knowledge of God, from which follows the doing of God's will. Men can receive genuine knowledge of God only through faith in Jesus Christ. It is the love of Christ that surpasses all knowledge and gives the power to do the will of God (Eph. 3:19). Love and knowledge are not to be separated. Knowledge leads to right conduct in love toward men, and true love opens up the dimensions of the fullness of God (Eph. 1:15 f.; 3:14-21). Connected with knowledge is the spirit of wisdom, which is something different from the spirit of intellectual perception. It takes wisdom to put the intellect into proper order and to translate it into fruitful and God-pleasing action. Such wisdom, however, is a gift of the Spirit of Christ residing in the hearts of the believers. Through this Spirit men are rooted and grounded in love.

Every instance of proclamation has as its goal to lead men to faith in God. In faith the forces of God's Word become fruitful and lead to a new life grounded in Jesus Christ. By faith the Gospel is passed on and thus becomes a reality and a power among men. Faith is the great fact that becomes visible as the Christians live together with their fellowmen, especially in a pagan environment. Through the power of faith the environment comes to life. Faith produces fruit, and it draws fellowmen into faith's reality. *No human suppositions are prerequisites for faith.* It arises solely from listening to the Word and using the sacraments; it lives in prayer and works in witness. In faith man knows God as his Lord and Redeemer. He trusts Him in all situations of life.

This faith is not limited to a few. Everyone is able to be brought to faith through God's Spirit. It is not dependent on race or social distinctions. Since God's love is the same for every man, the same faith arises through God's Word in all men.

Through faith Christ dwells in the hearts of the believers. Through faith men become capable of love and come to a proper understanding of God since He has revealed Himself in Jesus Christ in the immeasurable riches of His grace and of the gifts of His Spirit (Eph. 3:17 ff.). Since faith is the gift of God that gives everyone, regardless of social status, God's own resources, Paul does not praise his own faith and belittle that of others but always rejoices that he may receive again and again. *Faith is always open for the gift that others have to bestow.* This attitude of the apostle is highly characteristic. It stands in contrast to our theological and church practice that even today devaluates the faith of simple Christians because it objectifies faith in terms of the academic study of theology and judges it qualitatively according to theological knowledge. The Second Letter of Peter is addressed to "those who have obtained a faith of equal standing with ours in the righteousness of our God and Savior Jesus Christ" (1:1). On the basis of the New Testament, faith is no dead gift, no acceptance of truths, no sum of doctrinal statements, but a living, moving force flowing from trust in God and awakened by God's Word. God makes Himself the content of faith. The danger is always that Christians want to have faith as something they can control to their own edification. They are then concerned with themselves and do not let God's love animate them. They thereby limit the power of faith. Paul confronts this danger, for example, by praying for the Thessalonians that God "may fulfill every good resolve and work of faith by His power" (2 Thess. 1:11 f.). Thus faith becomes the fountain from which flows constantly new power for love. But faith also gives the hope that directs Christians beyond themselves, the power to stand the test of battle that can be waged only in view of the end. From hope grows peace in all conflict and joy in the Lord. In everything, however, the power of the Holy Spirit is revealed. (Rom. 15:13)

All these are gifts the congregations need for the sake of their service and which are mediated by faith. For this reason they are the object of Paul's intercession and thanksgiving. When he remembers his congregations, thanks and intercession often coalesce into each other (Eph. 1:15). *Whoever has eyes to see how God Himself is at work in the congregations can also pray for them aright* (Col. 1:4; 1 Thess. 1:3), *and when he does pray for them, he has the correct view of these associations.*

All mission work would be a senseless endeavor and every prayer would be self-deception if an *eternal goal* were not at stake, *which God has designated as the salvation of mankind* and which correspondingly must be proclaimed to all men. It is so decisive that Christians can think and act only in terms of their great hope of eternal life or in view of the coming Lord. They always live in profound responsibility toward the coming Lord. What the church does and what happens in mission has no goal in itself. Nor does it serve first of all to alleviate human needs. It is qualified and determined by the eternal inheritance that God has prepared for His own and promised to all men who come to faith in Him. This inheritance, in which redemption becomes a reality, is the Christians' great hope in which they are to rejoice (Rom. 12:12). It lies beyond every human realm. It is a gift of God. Consequently, God is a God of hope with something in the future prepared for His own. He is the redeeming God, and by virtue of what He has done for them in Jesus Christ He will bestow on them indestructible life in the resurrection of the dead. Therefore Paul prays that the Christians may not forget this goal. He prays God to grant that their hope by the power of the Holy Spirit may abound more and more (Rom. 15:13). This hope would not exist if Jesus Christ had not restored fellowship with the Father, if He had not by virtue of His resurrection become the content of the hope. He makes Christians steadfast in their hope (1 Thess. 1:3). On the basis of His resurrection they have a living hope, that is, an expectation that points and works toward the eternal goal, "an inheritance which is imperishable, undefiled, and unfading" (1 Peter 1:3 f.). It is not only what Jesus already has done that stands firm. What we may still expect because of His resurrection is also imperishable.

This hope distinguishes Christians from other men who have no hope and consequently have no genuine joy in their hearts. The certainty of hope makes Christians different people. It conditions their thinking, their living, their witness, and their suffering, and gives them the power of steadfastness. The content of hope is the goal of redemption. It always teaches us to look toward those who know nothing of it. Thus the congregation that lives in hope retains its missionary will. She can do nothing but speak of this glorious hope to all who still stand outside of it. On the other hand, whenever the eternal inheritance gets out of focus, overlaid with material goals and forced into the background, hope cannot develop its missionary power. Then comes failure in the Christian congregation. It accommodates itself to the world and thus no longer has any message for men. Its faith is powerless.

For this reason Christians must always remember the gift of salvation. Because of hope, faith remains lively. Thus practically all the passages about the apostle Paul's relationship to his congregations and those about his prayer life point toward the eternal inheritance. The intercession he makes is intent on not letting the saints grow forgetful about the component of hope in their calling, about the "riches of his glorious inheritance" (Eph. 1:18). The Christians' orientation to this common goal makes them "pure and blameless for the day of Christ" (Phil. 1:10). Therefore they should be joyfully "giving thanks to the Father, who has qualified us to share in the inheritance of the saints in light" (Col. 1:12). In view of this inheritance the Christian's entire life becomes a thanksgiving for what he has already received.

Since the eternal inheritance is with God, comes from Him, and is promised us by His love, it can be understood only as a gift of His love. No one can create his own inheritance. Hope for the gift of eternal life therefore guards the Christians against shaping their own redemption or taking into their own hands what God has given. God guards this inheritance in such a way that no one can take it over. He remains the Lord. Therefore it must be the Christians' concern to grasp in faith the gift promised to us in the justification of the sinner by grace. Man can do nothing but resign himself to the mercy of God and thank Him for His inexpressible gift. This feature is so striking in Paul that we get the impression that with reference to God all Paul knows is thanksgiving. Where he mentions prayer for the congregations he speaks of God in *an abundance of praise.* "Blessed be the God and Father of our Lord Jesus Christ, who has blessed us in Christ with every spiritual blessing in the heavenly places" (Eph. 1:3). He prays to the Father of glory (1:17). He is to be glorified in the church, and all generations are to join in the praise of God (3:21). The new life that comes from Christ is to serve "to the glory and praise of God" (Phil. 1:11). The release of the believers from sin and their removal from the evil age correspond with eternal life. Whoever gives God glory can no longer live in the kingdom of evil (Gal. 1:5). These facts are of such proportions that the congregations ought not to forget them anymore. Then the congregation can only join in the doxology that breaks forth from eternity and together with her flows into eternity (1 Tim. 1:17). Thus the church militant unites with the church triumphant in worship before the throne of God. (Rev. 4:11; 5:9; 7:12)

With this doxology mission gets its ultimate and most profound significance. It is a glorification of God via the church and leads to the glorification of God among the nations. Through the proclamation of His Gospel God gathers His church everywhere, and thus everywhere His praise arises.

Mission and prayer is a grand and weighty subject. We have designated it as the innermost thread of every life of prayer. Man in his existential needs is often moved so strongly by other concerns that he is in danger of forgetting the things of the kingdom of God, so that they take a back seat. And yet we must ask whether men's other concerns are properly ranked and can become a God-pleasing prayer if they are not subordinated to God's great goal. Not until the redemption of all men animates a man's heart can his own concerns find their proper significance before God. An individual can honor God only if he worships Him as the God of all mankind.

On the other hand, prayer for mission presupposes that the church practices prayer in the first place and that she is trained to practice a proper prayer life. She can pray for the mission only if she knows that she should pray at all times and that she may pray for all things. Prayer must therefore be a component part of her Christian life if she is to consider in prayer the grand concerns of the kingdom of God. Luther once designated prayer as the highest office of Christendom next to the preaching office. It is an office all Christians may practice. The more they learn to comprehend this, the more joyfully will Christianity put herself into God's service; all the more will she also see to it that the noblest office of all, the proclamation of the Gospel, will be practiced in all the world.

Bibliography

Asmussen, Hans. *Betet ohne Unterlass*, 1941.

Ebeling, Gerhard. *On Prayer* (nine sermons). Philadelphia: Fortress Press, 1966.

Hahn, Ferdinand. *Mission in the New Testament*. London: SCM Press, 1965.

Jeremias, Joachim. *The Lord's Prayer*. Philadelphia: Fortress Press (Facet Books, Biblical Series No. 8), 1964.

Lohmeyer, Ernst. *"Our Father": An Introduction to the Lord's Prayer*. New York: Harper & Row, 1965.

Luther, Martin. The Large Catechism in *The Book of Concord,* ed. Theodore G. Tappert. Philadelphia: Fortress Press, 1959.

Niles, D. T. *Upon the Earth: The Mission of God and the*

Missionary Enterprise of the Churches. New York: McGraw-Hill, 1962.

Schlatter, Adolf. *Kennen wir Jesus?* 1938.

Thielicke, Helmut. *Our Heavenly Father: Sermons on the Lord's Prayer*. New York: Harper & Brothers, 1960.